BIOLOGY MATTERS!

Volume 7
THE HUMAN BODY

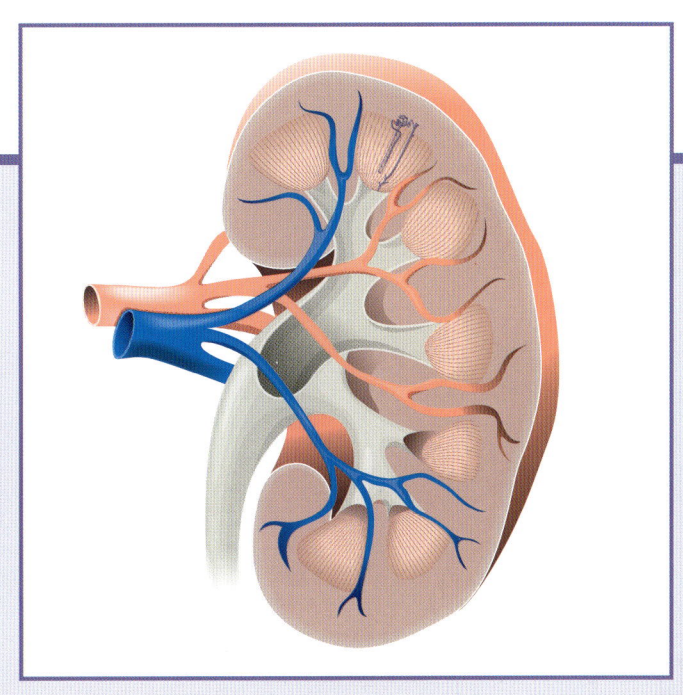

GROLIER

Published 2004 by Grolier
An imprint of Scholastic Library Publishing
Old Sherman Turnpike
Danbury, Connecticut 06816

© 2004 The Brown Reference Group plc

All rights reserved. Except for use in a review, no part of this book may be reproduced, stored in a retrieval system, or transmitted in any form, or by any means, electronic or mechanical, including photocopying, recording, or otherwise, without prior permission of Grolier.

FOR THE BROWN REFERENCE GROUP plc
Contributors: Patricia Davis, Robert Dinwiddy,
                      Ben Morgan, Natalie Goldstein,
                      Ian Wood, Chris Woodford
Consultant: Charles W. Holliday, Ph.D.
                      Dept of Biology, Lafayette College
Project Editor: Anne Wanjie
Deputy Editor: Jim Martin
Development Editor: Richard Beatty
Copy Editors: Lesley Campbell-Wright
                      John Jackson
Designer: Joan Curtis
Picture Researcher: Becky Cox
Illustrators: Darren Awuah, Richard Burgess,
                      Mark Walker
Indexer: Kay Ollerenshaw
Managing Editor: Bridget Giles
Design Manager: Lynne Ross
Production Director: Alastair Gourlay
Editorial Director: Lindsey Lowe

Printed and bound in Singapore

Volume ISBN 0-7172-5986-2
Set ISBN 0-7172-5979-X

Library of Congress Cataloging-in-Publication Data

Biology Matters!
    p. cm.
    Contents: v.1. Introduction to biology—v.2. Cell biology—v.3. Genetics—v.4. Microorganisms—v.5. Plants—v.6. Animals—v.7. The human body—v.8. Reproduction—v.9. Evolution—v.10. Ecology.
    ISBN 0-7172-5979-X (set : alk.paper)—ISBN 0-7172-5980-3 (v.1 : alk. paper)—ISBN 0-7172-5981-1 (v.2 : alk. paper)—ISBN 0-7172-5982-X (v.3 : alk. paper)—ISBN 0-7172-5983-8 (v.4 : alk. paper)—ISBN 0-7172-5984-6 (v.5 : alk. paper)—ISBN 0-7172-5985-4 (v.6 : alk. paper)—ISBN 0-7172-5986-2 (v.7 : alk. paper)—ISBN 0-7172-5987-0 (v.8 : alk. paper)—ISBN 0-7172-5988-9 (v.9 : alk. paper)—ISBN 0-7172-5989-7 (v.10 : alk. paper)
    1. Biology—Juvenile literature. [1. Biology.] I. Grolier Publishing Company

QH309.2.B56 2004
507—dc22

2003056942

ABOUT THIS SET

What could be more fascinating than the story of life? It is all told in *Biology Matters!* Across ten topical volumes this set reviews all fundamental life-science concepts. Each volume carefully introduces its topic, briefly examines the history, and fully displays all aspects of modern thinking about biology, ecology, evolution, genetics, cell biology, microbiology, life forms from every kingdom, and the human body. The clear text explains complex concepts and terms in full. Hundreds of photographs, artworks, and "Closeup" boxes provide details on key aspects. Simple, safe experiments encourage readers to explore biology in "Try This" boxes. "What Do You Think?" panels pose questions that test the reader's comprehension. "Applications" boxes show how biological knowledge enhances daily life and technology, while "Red Herring" boxes outline failed theories. "Hot Debate" panels illuminate the disagreements and discussions that rage in the biological sciences, and "Genetic Perspective" boxes outline the latest genetic research.

PICTURE CREDITS (b=bottom; t=top)
Front Cover: USDA: Ken Hammond.
The Brown Reference Group plc: 20, 21, 27, 33; **Corbis:** Joe Bator 16, Lester V. Bergman 38, 42b, 67, Gianni Dagli Orti 5, Charles O'Rear 59, Roger Ressmeyer 53, Jeffrey L. Rotman 10, Science Pictures Limited 42t, Ted Spiegel 70, David Woods 47; **Getty Images:** 31; **Imagingbody.com:** 15, 18, 29, 36, 58; **Ingram Publishing:** 50; **John Foxx Image Collection:** 32; **Mary Evans Picture Library:** 61; **NASA:** Jet Propulsion Library 55; **National Library of Medicine:** 6, 7; **PHIL:** 64; **Photodisc:** 26; **Rex Features:** 25, 52; **Science Photo Library:** 14, James Stevenson 65; **The Mira Foundation:** 56; **Topham:** 30 Novosti 34; **USDA:** Ken Hammond 9.

CONTENTS

Volume 7
The Human Body

Systems of the Body	4
Digestion and Excretion	8
Blood and Circulation	18
Breathing	26
Muscles and Bones	34
The Nervous System	44
Detecting the World	56
Health and Defense	64
Glossary	71
More Information	73
Set Index	74

1 Systems of the Body

Your body is made up of interconnected groups of organs and tissues that keep you alive, healthy, and working correctly. They are called the body's systems.

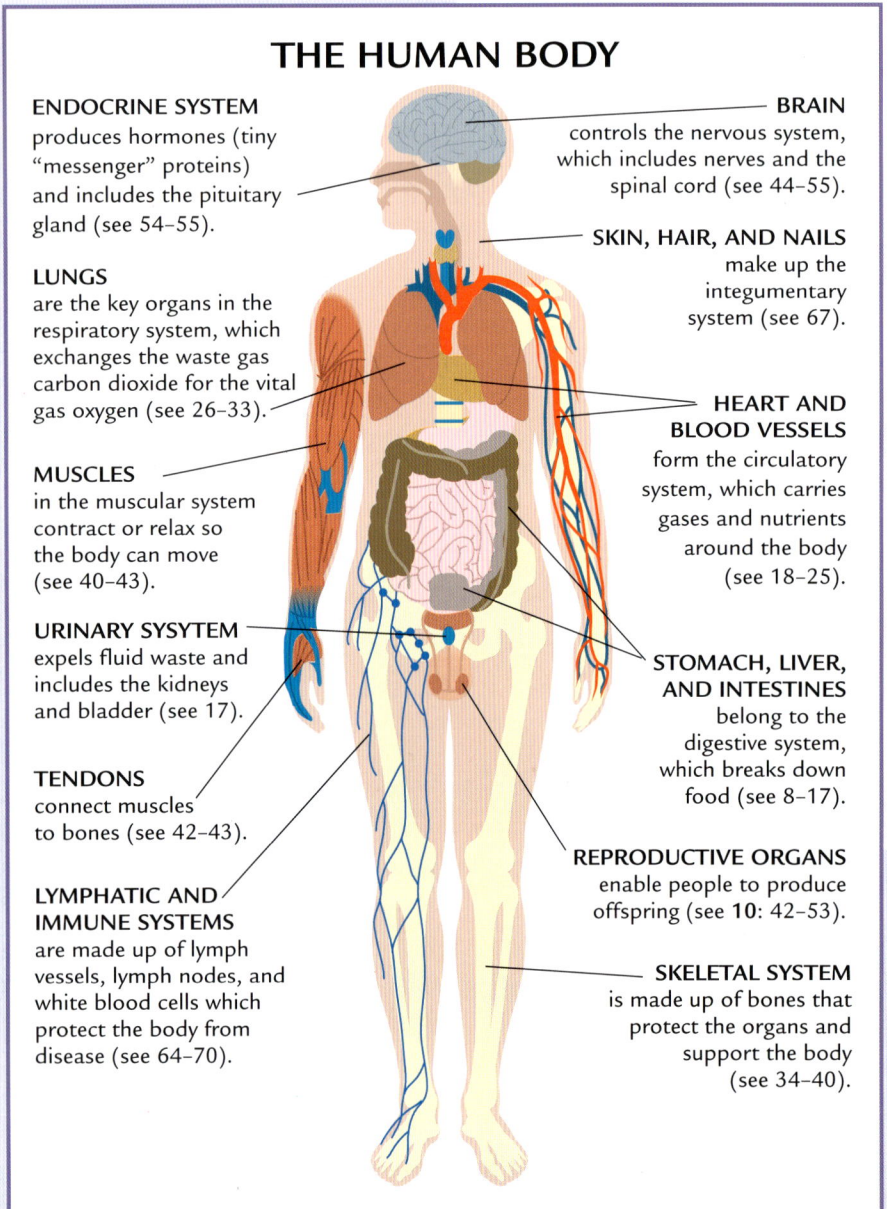

THE HUMAN BODY

ENDOCRINE SYSTEM produces hormones (tiny "messenger" proteins) and includes the pituitary gland (see 54–55).

LUNGS are the key organs in the respiratory system, which exchanges the waste gas carbon dioxide for the vital gas oxygen (see 26–33).

MUSCLES in the muscular system contract or relax so the body can move (see 40–43).

URINARY SYSYTEM expels fluid waste and includes the kidneys and bladder (see 17).

TENDONS connect muscles to bones (see 42–43).

LYMPHATIC AND IMMUNE SYSTEMS are made up of lymph vessels, lymph nodes, and white blood cells which protect the body from disease (see 64–70).

BRAIN controls the nervous system, which includes nerves and the spinal cord (see 44–55).

SKIN, HAIR, AND NAILS make up the integumentary system (see 67).

HEART AND BLOOD VESSELS form the circulatory system, which carries gases and nutrients around the body (see 18–25).

STOMACH, LIVER, AND INTESTINES belong to the digestive system, which breaks down food (see 8–17).

REPRODUCTIVE ORGANS enable people to produce offspring (see 10: 42–53).

SKELETAL SYSTEM is made up of bones that protect the organs and support the body (see 34–40).

The human body's systems begin to develop very early in life. An unborn baby starts off as just a single cell called a zygote. After the egg is fertilized by a sperm (see 8: 42–53), it splits into two identical cells. These two cells each divide again to make four cells, and then they divide to make eight cells, and so on over and over again (see 2: 60–61).

At first all the new cells are identical, but soon different kinds of cells start to appear. These cells form themselves into different types of tissues, which then develop into

Systems of the Body

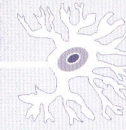

bone, muscle, and organs such as the heart and liver. The tissues and organs make up the basic parts of the body's systems. For example, organs such as the stomach and gut are part of the digestive system.

Major and minor systems
There are 10 systems in the human body. Six of them are called the major systems—not because they are more important than the others but because they extend through

GREEK ANATOMY

Until the 16th century most of the Western world's knowledge of human anatomy (the structure of the body and its systems) was based on the writings of the physician Claudius Galen (130–201 A.D.). Galen was born in Greece but worked in Rome, where he tried to figure out how the human body works by studying the insides of dead apes and pigs. Many of Galen's books about anatomy and medicine became the main source of information for medical students for more than a thousand years.

LEARNING FROM THE DEAD

The ancient Egyptians knew about the insides of the human body from the way they prepared their dead for burial, although their conclusions were not always correct. They removed the internal organs, stuffed the body with herbs and spices, and then soaked it in chemicals. This treatment mummified (preserved) the body by drying it so that it would not rot. The internal organs, sealed in separate jars of preserving spices, were placed in the tomb alongside the body.

A wall painting shows the ancient Egyptians purifying their dead before placing the bodies in a tomb.

BIOLOGY MATTERS! The Human Body

THE HEART OF THE MATTER

Flemish anatomist Andreas Vesalius (1514–1564) was one of the first scientists to study human anatomy by examining people's bodies. In 1543 he published a book called *On the Fabric of the Human Body*. This book caused an outcry because it questioned the works of Galen, still the basis of medical science at that time. But it inspired researchers all over Europe to take a fresh interest in anatomy, and their work eventually led to the downfall of Galen's theories.

◀ **Andreas Vesalius published his findings about human anatomy in the 16th century.**

▶ **The English physician William Harvey explains the circulation of blood to King Charles I in the 17th century.**

The last of Galen's ideas to bite the dust was about blood circulation. Galen thought that blood was produced by the liver and pumped around the body by the opening and closing of the blood vessels (the arteries and veins). The heart was where the blood mixed with air from the whole body. The major systems are the skeletal system (see 34–40), the muscular system (see 40–43), the circulatory system (the heart and blood vessels, see 18–25), the nervous system (the brain, spinal cord, and nerves; see 44–45), the integumentary system (the skin, see 67, hair, nails, and sweat glands) and the immune system (the cells in the blood that fight infection, see 66–70).

The other four systems—called the minor systems—are those inside the main body cavity, the chest and abdomen. The digestive system (see 8–17) includes the mouth, stomach, liver, and intestines. It converts food into energy and nutrients such as amino acids and sugars. The main part of the respiratory system is the lungs, which absorb oxygen from the air when you breathe in and expel carbon dioxide gas when you breathe out. The excretory system (see 17) includes the kidneys; the reproductive system (see **10**:

Systems of the Body

lungs. Until the 17th century most physicians accepted this theory. Then in 1628 the English physician William Harvey (1578-1657) published his discovery that the heart pumps blood out through the arteries, and the blood returns to the heart through the veins (see 22).

42–53) includes the reproductive organs; and the endocrine system (see 54–55) produces hormones (chemicals that help control all the other systems). Some organs are part of more than one of the body's systems. The pancreas, for example, is part of the digestive and endocrine systems.

 **INTO THE PAST**

SECRETS OF THE STOMACH

In 1822 a French Canadian named Alexis St. Martin was accidentally shot in the side, and the U.S. Army surgeon William Beaumont (1785-1853) treated him. The wound healed, but it left St. Martin with a permanent hole in his side that connected directly to his stomach. Beaumont realized that this was a chance to study how the stomach digests food. He tied pieces of meat, bread, and cabbage to the ends of silk strings and put them into St. Martin's stomach. A few hours later he pulled them out to see what had happened to them. In 1833 Beaumont published a description of how digestion works in the stomach.

CLOSEUP

HOMEOSTASIS

As well as doing their own jobs, systems work together to control the physical and chemical conditions inside the body. This process, called homeostasis, includes keeping the body at the correct temperature, around 98.6 °F (37.0 °C). Sweating cools the body, and shivering is a warming mechanism.

Other organs involved include the liver and pancreas, which control the concentration of sugar in the blood, and the kidneys, which control the body's water and salt content.

2 Digestion and Excretion

During digestion the body breaks down food into tiny particles that can dissolve in the blood. The particles are absorbed and carried to the body tissues. Excretion is the process by which the body gets rid of waste products after digestion.

▶ A healthy diet contains just a small amount of fat and sugar. It should also have plenty of dairy products, proteins such as meat and fish, vegetables and fruits, and carbohydrates such as bread and cereals.

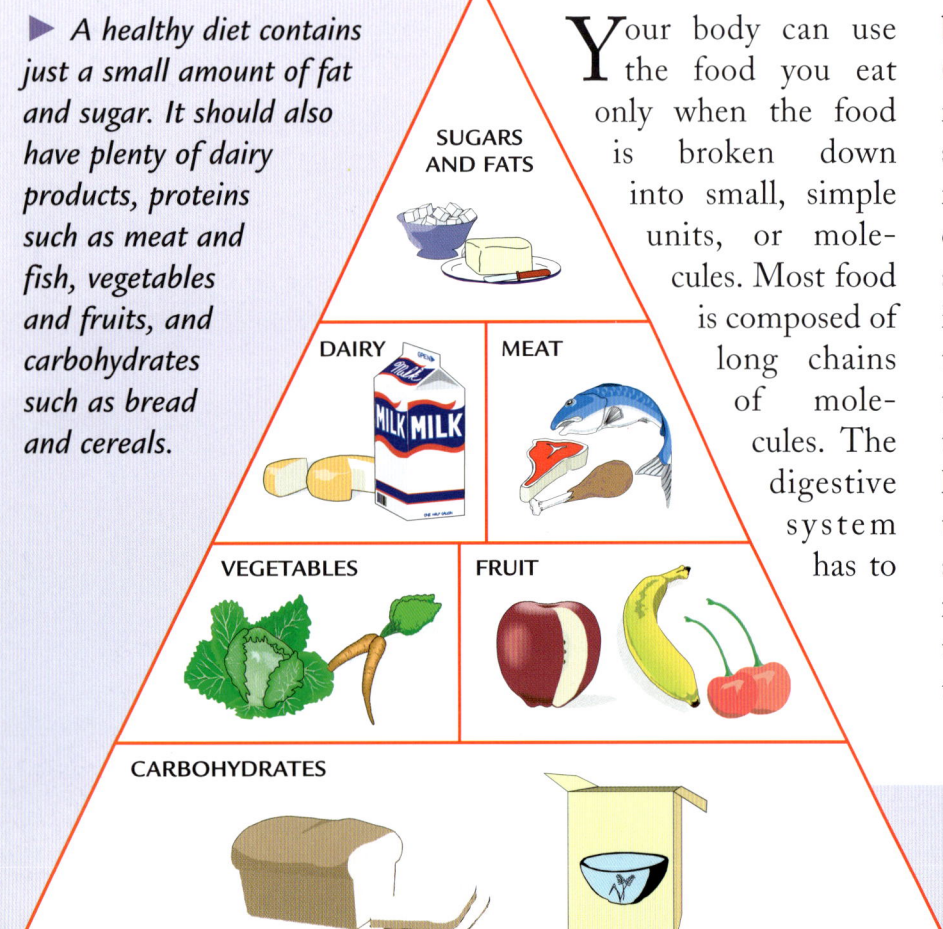

Your body can use the food you eat only when the food is broken down into small, simple units, or molecules. Most food is composed of long chains of molecules. The digestive system has to break the links in the chains (see **1**: 28–37). This process reduces the large molecules to smaller ones, which are carried by the blood to the body's cells. The cells use them as fuel or reassemble them into new chains, forming the building blocks for new tissues. The chemical reactions inside the cells produce lots of waste products, which the blood carries away. Wastes are destroyed and removed from the body by organs in the excretory system, such as the kidneys, and by the liver.

Digestion and Excretion

FOOD AND DIET

To stay healthy, the human body needs a continual supply of food to provide energy and chemical building blocks for growing new tissues and repairing damaged ones. There are three main types of food that you need to eat—proteins, carbohydrates, and fats. You also need to take in water, fiber, and small amounts of important substances called vitamins and minerals.

Proteins build muscles and create a vast range of complex chemicals inside the body's cells. They come from foods such as meat, cheese, fish, eggs, beans, and nuts. During digestion they break down into tiny molecules called amino acids, which dissolve in the blood and are carried around the body to where they are needed.

Carbohydrates provide a quick energy source. Complex carbohydrates, such as starch, come from foods such as rice and potatoes. Simple carbohydrates, or sugars, come from sweet foods and fruit juices. During digestion carbohydrates are broken down into molecules called monosaccharides (see **1**: 30–31). Body cells use carbohydrates to fuel the chemical reactions within

▲ *A well-balanced diet contains all the important food types. This is essential if you are to grow properly and have enough energy and strength for working and playing.*

CLOSEUP: DIETARY FIBER

Not everything you eat is digested. Dietary fiber, or roughage, is the name for all sorts of tough plant materials that the body cannot digest. Although your body does not digest fiber, it is an important part of your diet. It absorbs water and so adds bulk to food. That helps the digestive system push the food along the digestive tract. If you do not have enough fiber in your food, you might get disorders of the digestive system such as constipation or diarrhea.

▲ This boy is suffering from a disease called rickets. It is caused by having too little vitamin D in the diet. Vitamin D helps the body take up calcium from food. Calcium makes bones healthy and strong. Many children with rickets have soft bones, which makes their legs bow outward.

the cells. If you eat more carbohydrates than you need, the leftovers are turned into fat for storage.

Foods such as butter, oil, cheese, and chocolate are rich in fats. Fats contain twice as much energy per ounce as carbohydrates do, and so they provide a valuable long-term supply of energy for the body. They are also needed for making essential substances, including chemicals called hormones (see 54–55), which control processes in the body, and the molecules that form cell membranes. During digestion fats are broken down into particles called fatty acids, monoglycerides, and glycerol. Fats can also be used as a valuable supply of energy for the body.

Vitamins and minerals are important for keeping you healthy, but only very small amounts of most are required. Vitamins are a group of complex organic (carbon-containing) substances that play a key role in certain chemical reactions in the body. Vitamin A, for example, is essential for the normal growth of bones and teeth. It is also important for vision and helps you see in the dark.

Minerals are simple, inorganic compounds (ones that do not contain carbon) such as sodium and iron. Minerals

Digestion and Excretion

▶ *The human digestive system. The sections of the small intestine absorb food and further break down the food. The large intestine is mainly important for retrieving water from the remnants of the food.*

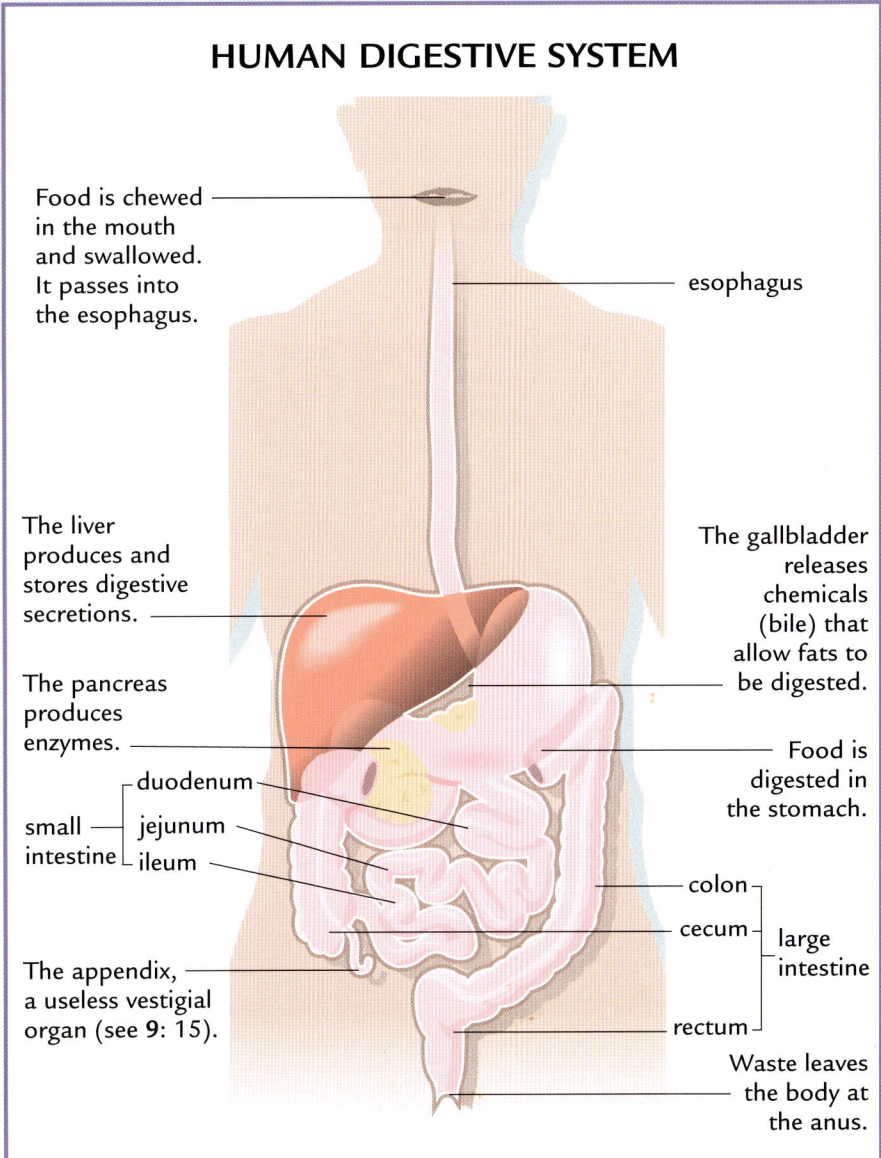

also play important roles in body chemistry. Iron, for example, is needed to make hemoglobin, a chemical that binds to oxygen and is carried through the body by red blood cells (see 30–31).

DIGESTION

Food is detected and analyzed by sense organs (see 62–63) before and after it enters the mouth. There the food is chewed, and saliva begins to break it down. The food then passes through a long tube, called the digestive tract. In this tract chemicals called

CLOSEUP

ENZYMES

Enzymes (see **1**: 34–35) are proteins that speed up chemical reactions in the body. Cells contain thousands of different types of enzymes, each of which controls a particular reaction.

Digestive enzymes work outside cells, inside the organs of the digestive system. They speed up a chemical reaction called hydrolysis, in which water molecules attack chain molecules (see **1**: 29–35) and break apart the links. Digestive enzymes are produced in the mouth, stomach, small intestine, and pancreas. Examples of digestive enzymes are the proteases, which break down proteins into amino acids.

enzymes attack the food and break it down further. The remains of food that have not been digested finally leave the body through an opening called the anus.

The mouth

The process of digestion begins before you even eat anything. The sight and smell of food trigger the release of a slimy fluid called saliva, which moistens the food once it is in the mouth, making it easier to chew and swallow. The saliva also contains an enzyme that begins to break down a type of carbohydrate in the food called starch.

The powerful muscles of the jaw work together with

TEETH

People have 32 teeth, of which there are four different types: Incisors at the front for cutting, canines for piercing, and premolars and molars at the back for cutting and grinding. The white, visible part of a tooth is called the crown. It is covered with a substance called enamel, which is the hardest material in the human body. Under the enamel is a hard layer of dentine, and under it is the pulp cavity, which contains blood vessels and nerves. Each tooth is anchored into the jawbone by roots.

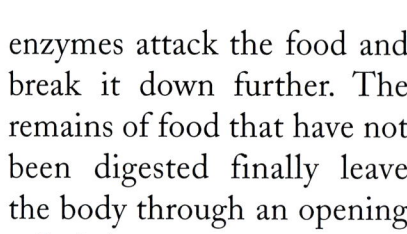

The same series of teeth appear on each side of the jaw.

Digestion and Excretion

the teeth to cut and mash the food until it is soft and moist enough to swallow. Taste buds on the tongue detect the four main tastes in food—salty, bitter, sweet, and acidic (see 63). Gases released by the warm food travel into the nose, where their smell contributes to the flavor. When you swallow your food, it travels down a tube called the esophagus to the stomach. The food does not simply fall into the stomach. It is pushed along the esophagus by waves of muscular squeezing (contraction) called peristalsis.

The stomach

The stomach is a stretchy muscular bag that expands as it fills up. Food spends up to four hours in the stomach being churned around by contractions of the muscles in the stomach wall. The lining of the stomach produces a digestive liquid called gastric juice. It contains an enzyme

HOW SALIVA WORKS

You can learn the effects of enzymes for yourself by chewing some food. Put a piece of bread in your mouth, and chew it for 30 seconds. As the bread mixes with your saliva, it will start to taste sweeter. That happens because an enzyme called salivary amylase breaks down the carbohydrate starch into a sugar called maltose.

PERISTALSIS

The walls of the digestive system are made up of two layers of smooth muscle. One layer is arranged lengthways, and the other is arranged in rings. These muscles contract in a rhythmic way, causing the food to be pushed slowly along the digestive system. This action, called peristalsis, causes some of the gurgling noises and movements you can sometimes feel in your belly.

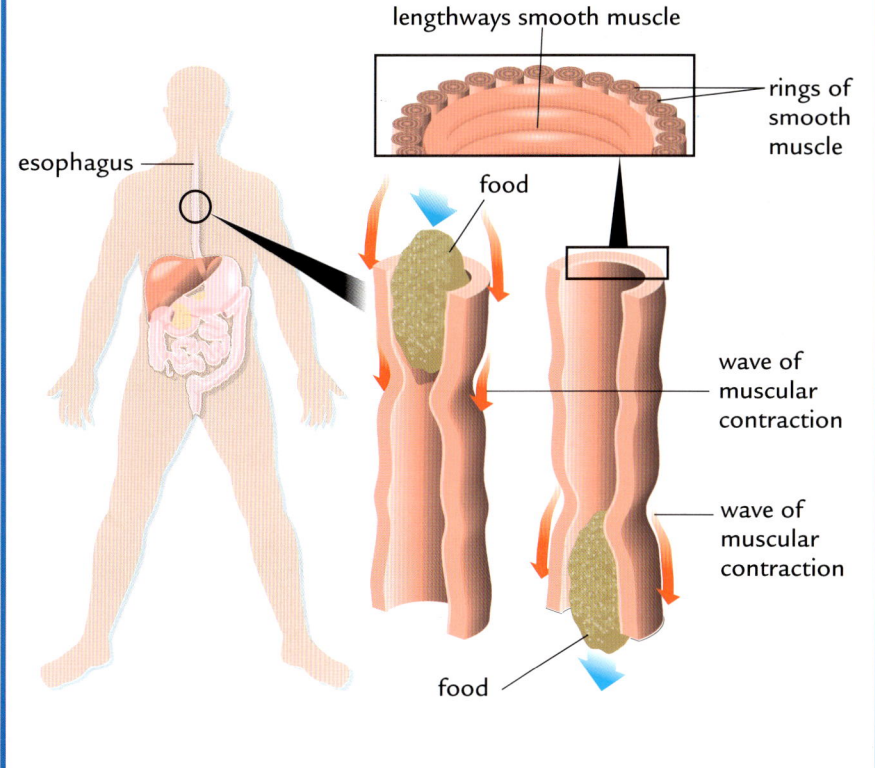

BIOLOGY MATTERS! The Human Body

EMULSIFICATION

TRY THIS

Pour a little vegetable oil into two glasses of warm water. Add soap liquid to one glass, then stir both of them quickly for around 10 seconds. The mixture containing soap liquid will form a milky fluid, but the other mixture will slowly separate back into layers of water and oil.

Fats and oils do not mix with water easily. They separate out as globules, which makes them difficult to digest. In the small intestine bile breaks down these globules by emulsifying them—it turns them into thousands of much tinier droplets. Soap liquid works in the same way bile does.

called pepsin, which breaks down proteins in food, as well as hydrochloric acid, which kills germs and helps pepsin work by attacking proteins.

The stomach reduces the food to a creamy liquid, and contractions then squirt the fluid out of an opening called the pyloric sphincter into the first part of the small intestine, called the duodenum. Sphincters are rings of muscle that can open and close.

The small intestine

Most digestion takes place in the small intestine. In the duodenum food from the stomach mixes with two digestive juices—bile from the liver and pancreatic juice from the pancreas. Bile helps the digestion of fats by making larger droplets of liquid fat break down into microscopic droplets. This process is called emulsification. Bile is stored in a small sac called the gallbladder. Pancreatic juice contains many enzymes that digest proteins, carbohydrates, and fats. These enzymes continue working throughout the small intestine.

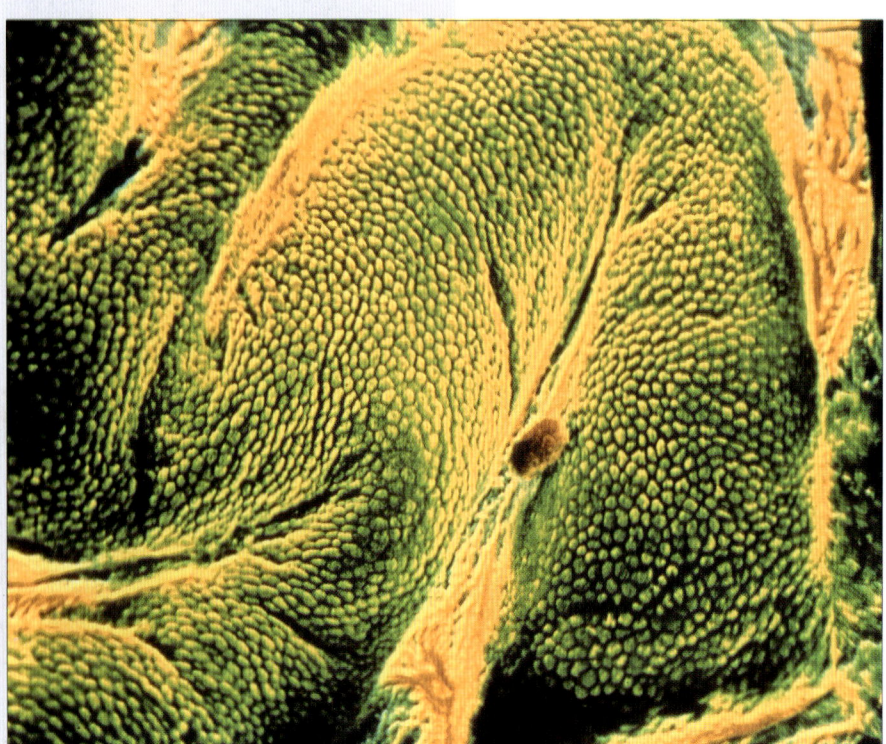

▼ The bile duct wall, magnified many times. This duct takes bile to the small intestine from the gallblader.

Digestion and Excretion

WHY DO DIGESTIVE SYSTEMS NOT DIGEST THEMSELVES?

The lining of the stomach and intestines would be digested if it were not well protected. Glands within it produce a thick fluid called mucus that protects the lining and makes it slippery, helping food move along. Even so, the walls of the digestive system suffer a lot of wear and tear, so they have to grow a new lining continually, just as skin does. Dead cells rub off the top of the lining and are carried away and digested.

As a meal travels along the small intestine, most of the food within it is digested into small molecules. These molecules then pass across the lining of the intestine and enter the bloodstream to be carried away to the body's cells. The small intestine's lining has many fingerlike folds called villi (sing. villus) over its surface. They are covered by even tinier projections called microvilli. Inside each villus is a network of blood vessels (capillaries) with very thin walls, which pick up small molecules from digested food.

The large intestine

Undigested food enters the large intestine, which absorbs water and leaves behind a semisolid material. Harmless bacteria feed on this waste matter. They break down some of the fiber, releasing sugar and some vitamins, which are then absorbed by the body. The bacteria also produce hydrogen, methane, and carbon dioxide gas, which can build up and cause wind.

Waste matter spends up to two days in the large intestine. It collects as a material called feces in a part of the digestive tract called the rectum. The feces are pushed out by muscles in the rectum.

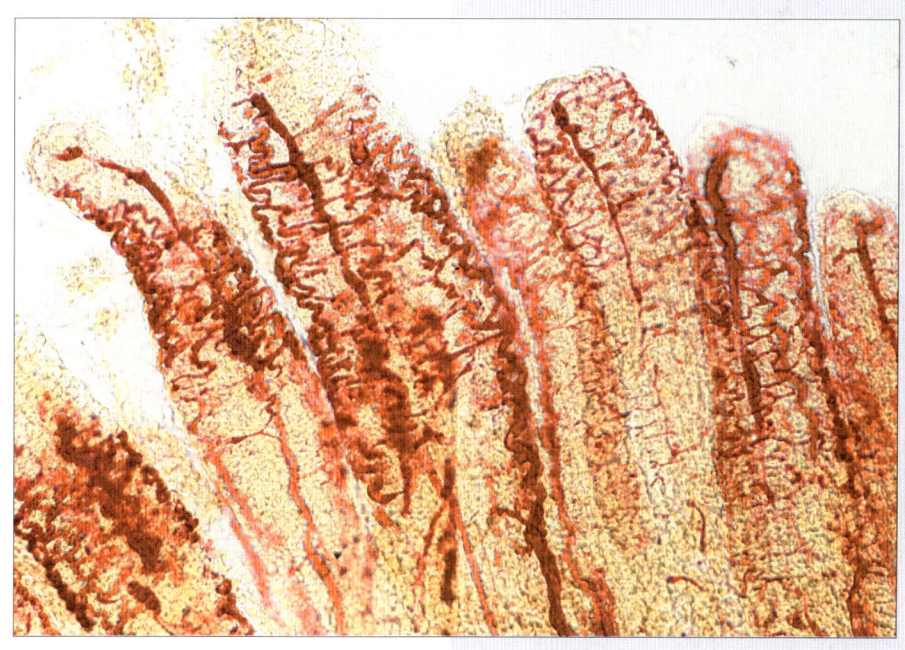

▼ Fingerlike folds called villi cover the lining of the small intestine. The villi make the surface area much bigger than it would otherwise be, so there is a large area over which food molecules can be absorbed.

BIOLOGY MATTERS! The Human Body

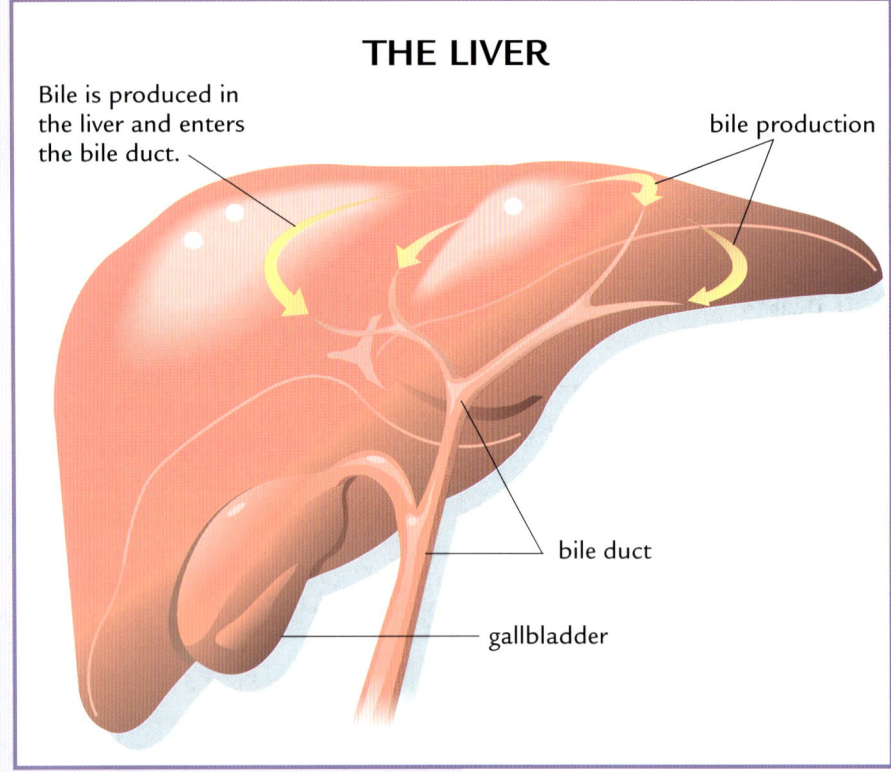

THE LIVER

Bile is produced in the liver and enters the bile duct.

bile production

bile duct

gallbladder

The liver

The bloodstream carries digested food away from the intestines and to an organ called the liver. The liver works like a chemical factory. It carries out hundreds of tasks that keep the concentrations of sugar, amino acids, and various other chemicals in the blood just right. Excess food and iron are removed and stored in the liver for later. A sugar called glucose is turned into a carbohydrate called glycogen, which can be quickly broken down and released again as glucose when it is needed in the body.

The liver also destroys poisons, such as alcohol, that enter the body with food. The liver manufactures vitamin A, breaks down worn-out blood cells, and creates bile.

◄ *A newborn baby receives phototherapy to treat jaundice, a problem that occurs when the liver makes too much bile.*

Digestion and Excretion

The kidneys

The kidneys are two organs in the lower back shaped like large beans. They are the main organs of excretion. They continually filter the blood, removing water and chemical wastes. Each kidney contains about one million individual tubes called nephrons.

Blood enters each nephron through a knot of tiny blood vessels called a glomerulus. The glomerulus works just like a sieve. It allows water and other small molecules (including salts, sugars, and chemical wastes such as urea) to leave the blood and enter a long, looped tube called a renal tubule. The renal tubule is surrounded by even more tiny blood vessels. As the filtered blood moves through the renal tubule, sugars and salts are taken back into the blood, along with water. At the same time, waste molecules are left in the nephron or secreted into it.

More than 99 percent of the fluid entering the nephron from the blood is taken back into the body. The rest drains out of the nephrons through collecting ducts. It leaves the kidneys and passes along tubes called ureters to collect in the bladder. At this point the fluid is called urine. When the bladder fills up, it sends a nerve signal to the brain, causing the feeling of wanting to urinate (pass water).

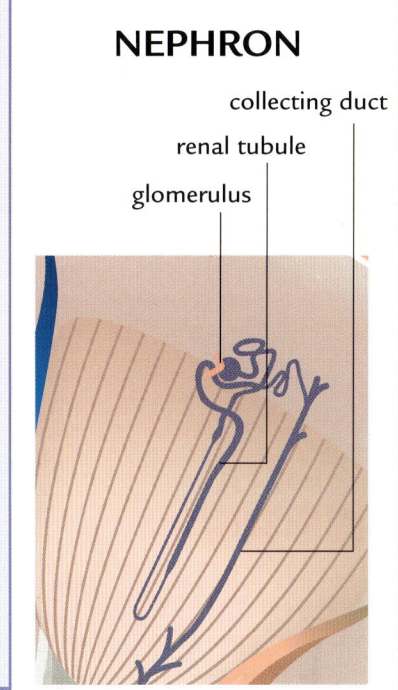

NEPHRON
- collecting duct
- renal tubule
- glomerulus

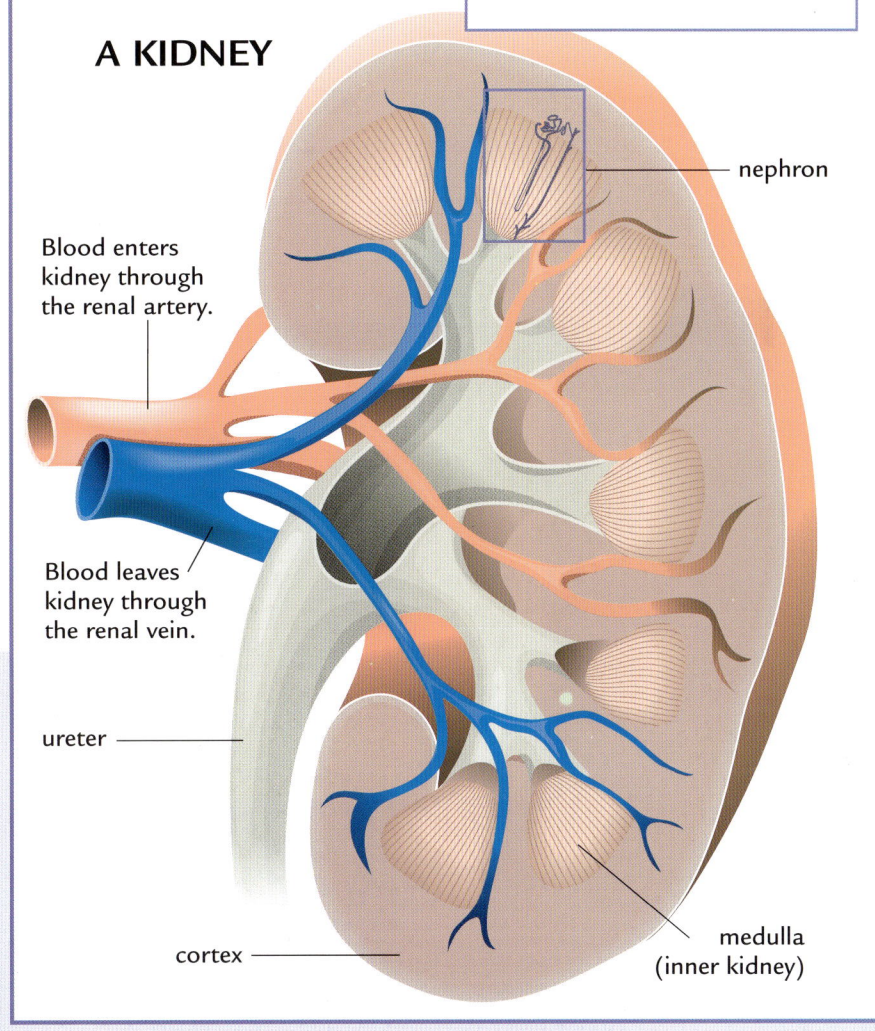

A KIDNEY
- nephron
- Blood enters kidney through the renal artery.
- Blood leaves kidney through the renal vein.
- ureter
- cortex
- medulla (inner kidney)

3 Blood and Circulation

▼ *A surgeon holds a human heart, which will be transplanted into a patient whose own heart is not working properly. During the operation the patient is connected to a heart bypass machine, which adds oxygen to the blood and pumps it around the body while the new heart is attached.*

The circulatory system is all the tubes and channels (blood vessels) through which blood flows and the heart, which pumps blood around the body.

The blood vessel system is like a many-branched vine. The largest blood vessels enter and leave the heart. They get smaller and smaller as they branch out to reach all the body cells. The blood and circulatory system are essential in transporting oxygen (see 26–33), nutrients (see 8–17), and waste materials around the body. The system also helps coordinate all the other body systems (see 4–7). The blood is also part of the immune (defense) system. It contains white blood cells that help fight infection by microorganisms (see 66–70).

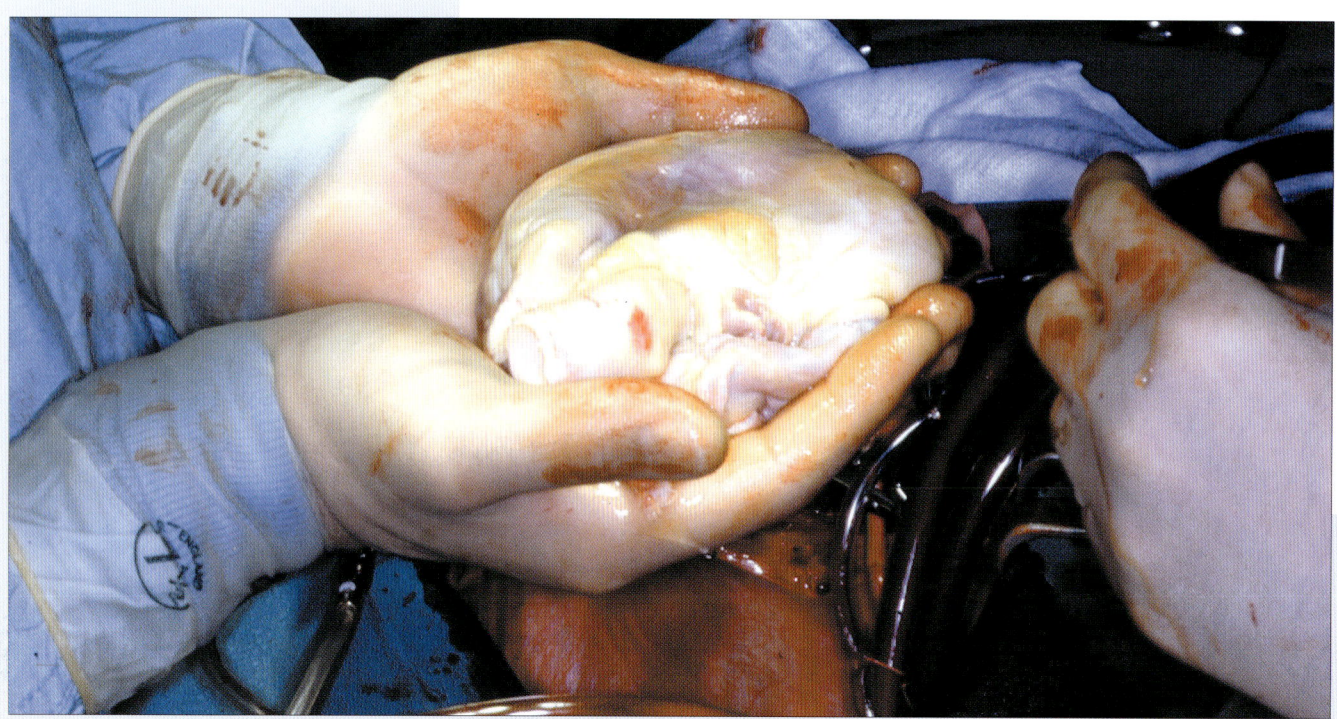

Blood and Circulation

The heart

Most of the time you are not aware of your heart. However, when you exercise or when you are frightened or angry, you can feel it beating powerfully and sense the blood pounding in your head. The heart is the engine of the circulatory system, which supplies all parts of your body with blood.

The heart is a pump located in the center of your chest. It has four hollow chambers; the top two are called atria (singular, atrium), and the two at the bottom are called ventricles. The heart's structure and function are so unique that many of its workings are still not well understood.

The tissue that makes up the heart is called cardiac muscle (see 41–42). Like the smooth muscle that surrounds hollow organs, such as the

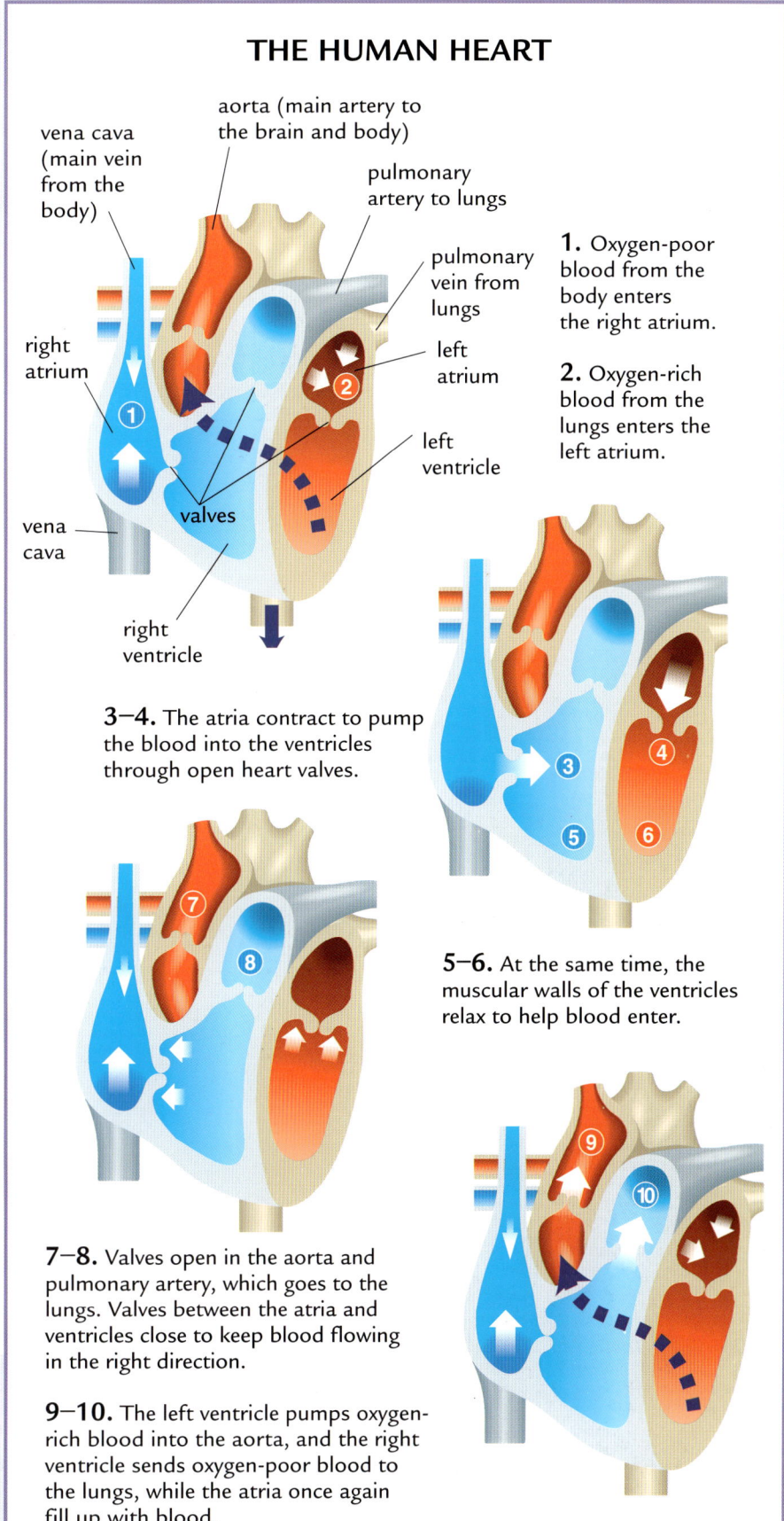

THE HUMAN HEART

1. Oxygen-poor blood from the body enters the right atrium.

2. Oxygen-rich blood from the lungs enters the left atrium.

3–4. The atria contract to pump the blood into the ventricles through open heart valves.

5–6. At the same time, the muscular walls of the ventricles relax to help blood enter.

7–8. Valves open in the aorta and pulmonary artery, which goes to the lungs. Valves between the atria and ventricles close to keep blood flowing in the right direction.

9–10. The left ventricle pumps oxygen-rich blood into the aorta, and the right ventricle sends oxygen-poor blood to the lungs, while the atria once again fill up with blood.

BIOLOGY MATTERS! The Human Body

TRY THIS — LISTENING TO YOUR HEARTBEAT

A stethoscope is an instrument used to listen to the heartbeat. In 1819 the French physician René Laënnec (1781–1826) made the first stethoscope out of a hollow wooden tube 1 inch (2.5cm) wide and 10 inches (25cm) long.

You can use a cardboard tube from the inside of a roll of paper towels to make a stethoscope. Work with a partner. Put one end of the tube high in the center of your partner's chest. Put your ear against the other end. Do you hear the "lubb-dubb" of the heartbeat? Count the number of heartbeats you hear in 30 seconds. Multiply by 2 to get the number of beats in 1 minute. That is your partner's heartbeat rate.

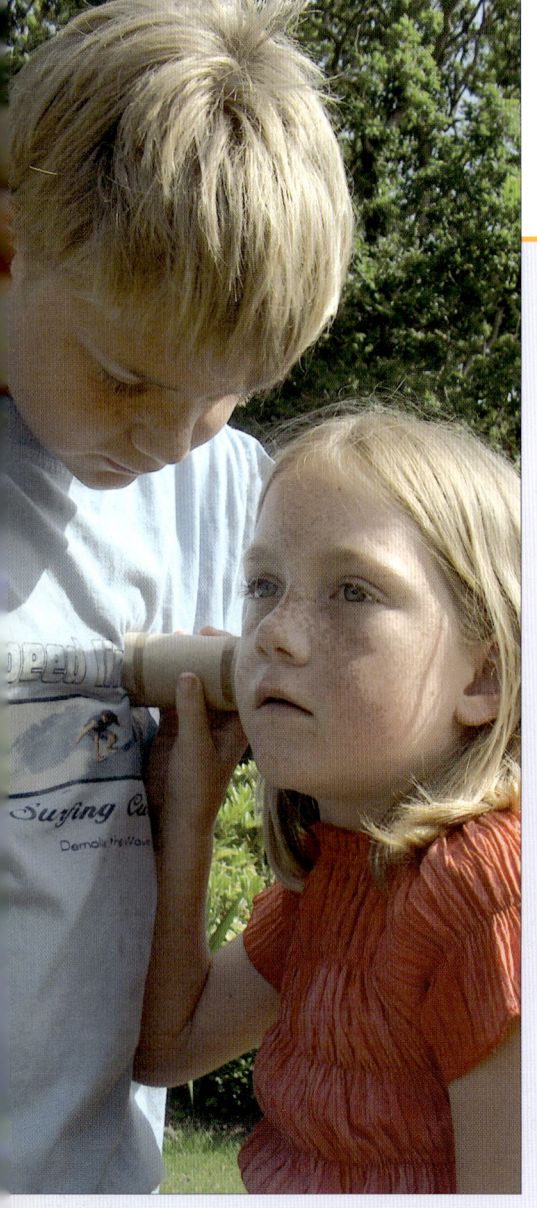

intestines, cardiac muscle can squeeze (contract) involuntarily—you do not have to "tell" your heart muscle to work; it does it automatically. Yet, like the muscles attached to your bones (skeletal muscles), heart muscle is striated (made of long fibers). So, cardiac muscle is a cross between smooth muscle and skeletal muscle.

◀ Listen carefully and count the number of heartbeats you can hear for a given length of time. A 12-year-old's heart usually beats around 85 times every minute, but this rate is more than doubled after strenuous exercise.

Cardiac muscle also has unique connections between its cells that help all the heart's muscle cells contract rapidly and at the same time.

On average, the adult heart beats around 72 times per minute. Around 3 fluid ounces (80ml) of blood are pumped into the main artery with each beat, so the heart usually pumps up to 1½ gallons (7 liters) of blood per minute. During strenuous exercise such as running, that can rise to 6 gallons (27 liters) per minute in an average adult.

Heart control

Perhaps the most amazing feature of the heart is that it can control some of its own actions without any outside regulation, even from the brain. Tiny electrical impulses or bursts regulate the pumping of various parts of the heart. These impulses come from areas within the heart called nodes.

Blood and Circulation

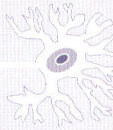

The sinoatrial (or SA) node is located on the wall of the right atrium. The impules sent from the SA node regulate the heartbeat. So the SA node is called the heart's pacemaker. Another node, called the atrioventricular (AV) node, slows the SA node impulses enough to allow the atria to finish contracting before the ventricles begin contracting. The impulses are sent rapidly to cardiac cells in the ventricles through cardiac muscle strands called Purkinje fibers.

People with a slow or irregular heartbeat can have a pacemaker put in their chest to control the beat (see **1**: 65).

The rhythmic contraction of heart muscles produces the "lubb-dubb" sound of the heartbeat. The "lubb" sound is when the atria have finished contracting, the atrial valves close, and the ventricles begin to contract. The "dubb" sound occurs when the ventricles have pumped out blood, and the valves between the ventricles and the arteries close.

Blood flow through the heart

Blood enters both atria at almost the same time from large blood vessels. They are the vena cavae, which carry oxygen-poor, or deoxygenated, blood from the body, and the pulmonary blood vessels, which carry oxygen-rich, or oxygenated, blood from the

TRY THIS
CHECKING YOUR PULSE

To check how fast your heart is beating, ask a partner to put two fingers on your wrist artery to feel your pulse. It is on the inside of your wrist. Use a stopwatch to count the number of pulses in 15 seconds. First, take your pulse when you are sitting and resting. Then, run for two minutes. Immediately after, take your pulse for 15 seconds. Multiply each number by 4 to get the number of pulses per minute. How much faster was your heart beating after you ran than when you were resting?

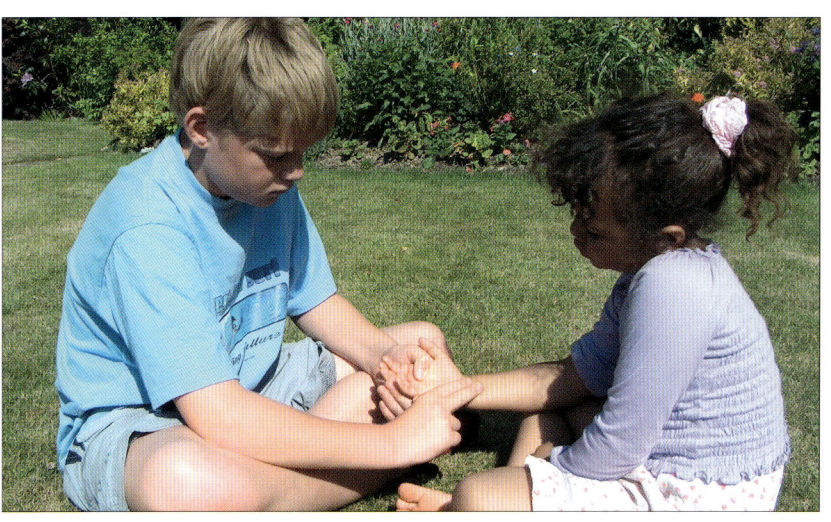

BIOLOGY MATTERS! The Human Body

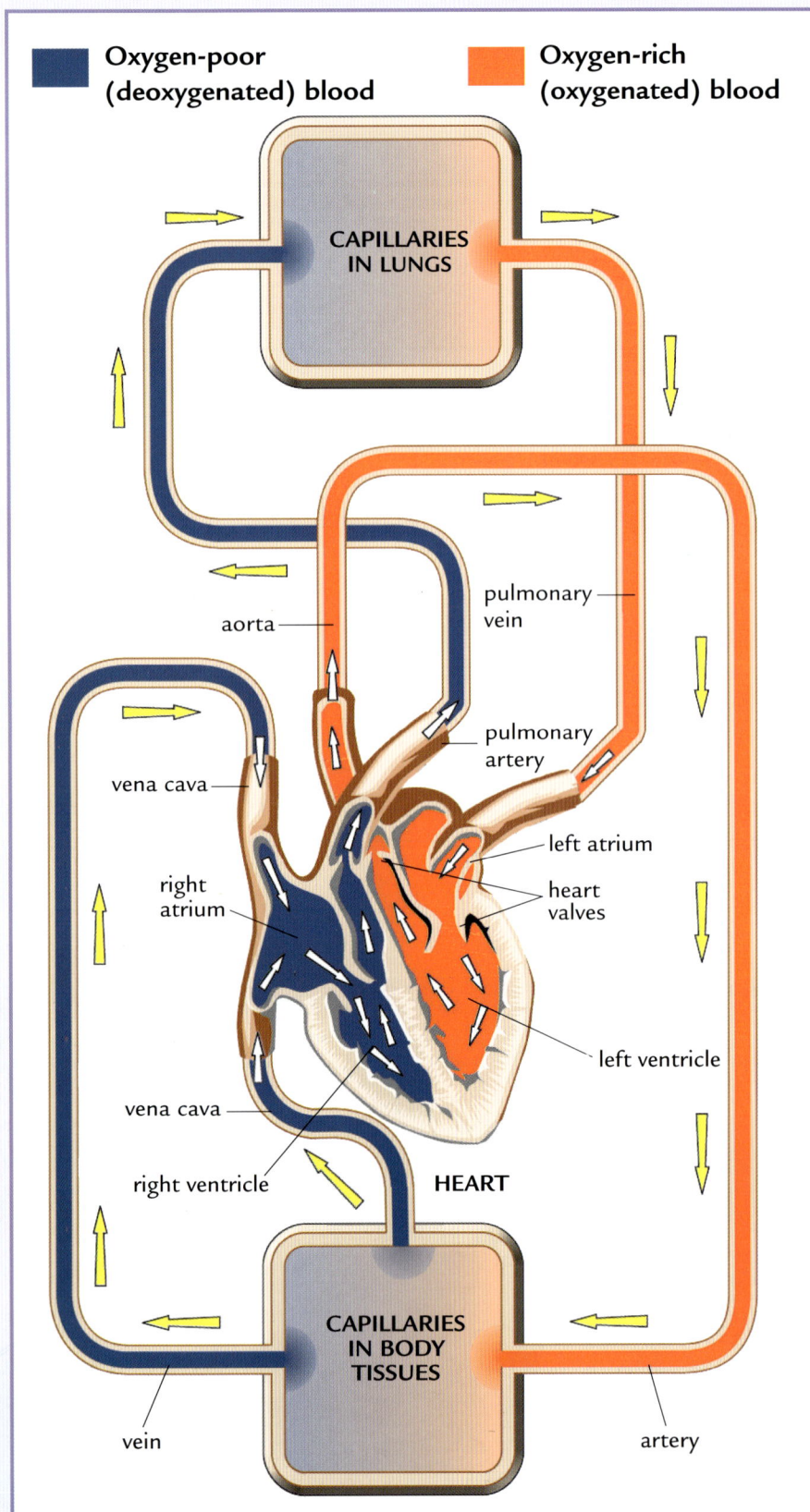

▼ Deoxygenated blood from the body goes to the right side of the heart. It is pumped to the lungs, where it offloads carbon dioxide and picks up oxygen. Oxygenated blood goes to the left side of the heart and is pumped around the body.

lungs back to the heart. Oxygen-poor blood enters the right atrium. Oxygen-rich blood from the lungs enters the left atrium.

The atria contract to pump the blood into the ventricles. When blood enters the atria, the ventricles are empty. The thick, muscular walls of the ventricles relax, increasing their volume and pulling in blood through the atria from the veins. The atria then contract to pump the ventricles full of blood. Both ventricles then contract forcefully. The right ventricle pumps blood into arteries that carry it to the lungs to pick up oxygen. At the same time, the left ventricle pumps its oxygen-rich blood into the aorta—a large blood vessel that channels the blood to the brain and the rest of the body.

Valves between the heart chambers keep the blood flowing in the correct direction.

Blood and Circulation

HEART TRANSPLANTS

Some people with diseased hearts can be saved by transplanting a healthy heart into their body. There are not enough human hearts available, however. This has led surgeons to experiment with implanting baboon hearts into people. Many people are worried by such procedures; what if baboon viruses or other diseases are passed on to humans? Some people believe that transplanting organs from one species to another raises questions about what it means to be human. Are you still human if one of your vital organs is nonhuman? Others suggest that breeding animals to kill them for their organs is wrong. Supporters say that such experiments may save many lives.

The valve between the right atrium and ventricle is called the tricuspid valve. After the right atrium pumps blood into the right ventricle, the tricuspid valve closes. That stops the blood from flowing back into the atrium. The bicuspid, or mitral, valve does the same for the left atrium. The veins also have one-way valves that allow blood to flow only toward the heart.

Blood circulation

Blood vessels carry blood to nearly all the cells in the body. The aorta and other blood vessels attached directly to the heart are the body's largest blood vessels. The next largest are the major arteries, which branch into various parts of the body. Smaller blood vessels, called arterioles, branch off the arteries and get smaller and smaller, eventually forming a web of minute tubes that carry blood to every body cell. These smallest blood vessels are called capillaries, which are tubes with walls only one cell thick. A mass of capillaries in a piece of tissue is called a capillary bed.

Oxygen in the blood moves from the capillaries into the cells. In return the cells release carbon dioxide as waste into the capillaries.

▼ A capillary bed (1)—the site of gas exchange in the body's tissues—lies between a vein (2) and an artery (3). The arteries and arterioles (small arteries, 4) bring oxygenated blood to the capillary bed from the heart, while the venules (small veins, 5) and veins take deoxygenated blood back to the heart.

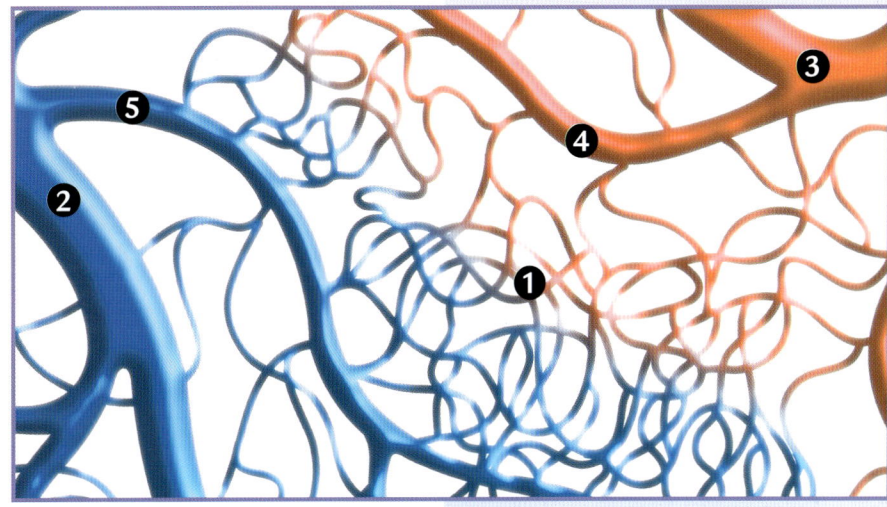

BIOLOGY MATTERS! The Human Body

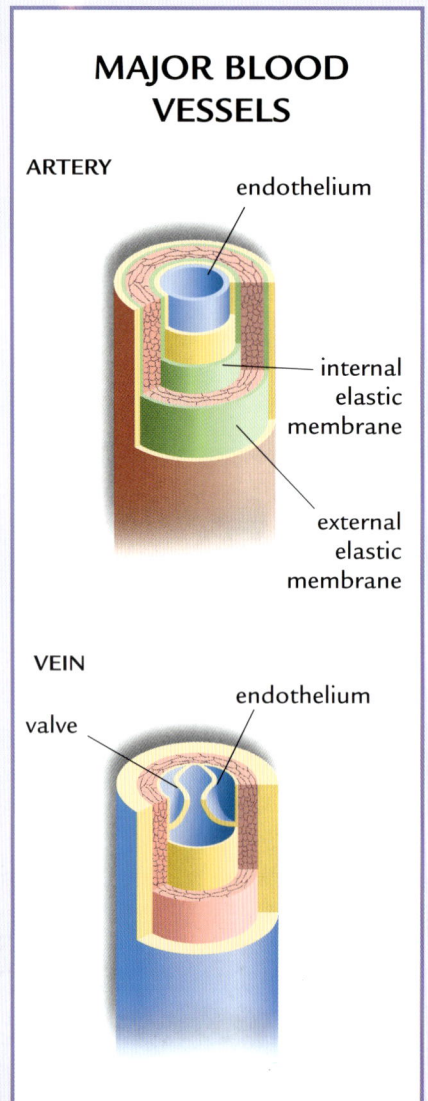

MAJOR BLOOD VESSELS

◀ *Arteries receive blood from the heart. They have elastic fibers so they can withstand high pressures. Veins return blood to the heart. Some have valves to stop backflow.*

This process, called gas exchange, occurs at the capillary bed. The capillaries that receive carbon dioxide are the beginning of the system of veins that carries oxygen-poor blood back to the heart (see 29–33). Like the arteries, as veins approach the heart, they become larger. The vena cavae (singular, vena cava) are the largest veins. Veins are lined with one-way flap valves that keep the blood moving toward the heart, which is why blood does not gather in your feet.

The smooth muscles of the arteries near where they join with the capillaries expand or contract to regulate blood flow to different areas of the body. After you eat, arterioles carrying blood to the capillary beds of the stomach and intestines open to allow more blood to flow to the digestive tract (see 13–15). Arterioles in the arms and legs may contract and restrict blood flow during digestion. When it is hot outside, you may look "flushed" because arterioles near the skin surface open to allow more blood to flow to your skin, cooling it. When it is cold, you often look "drawn" because arterioles in the skin contract to limit blood flow and heat loss.

The blood

The blood carries oxygen and nutrients to all body cells and removes wastes from them. There are many types of blood cells, each with a distinct job to do. The clear liquid that carries all the blood cells is called plasma. There is about 1 gallon (5 liters) of blood in an adult's body. Red blood cells contain a substance called hemoglobin,

WHAT DO YOU THINK?

HEART DISEASE

Heart disease is one of the leading causes of death in the United States. One major cause of heart disease is atherosclerosis. This condition is the accumulation in the arteries of fatty deposits rich in cholesterol. Fatty meat is by far the food that contributes most to atherosclerosis.

Some people have suggested that the government put a tax on meat to discourage people from eating it. Like the tax on tobacco, this fee could improve the health of millions of Americans and encourage them to eat more healthful whole grains instead of animal fat. What do you think of this suggestion?

TYPES OF WHITE BLOOD CELLS

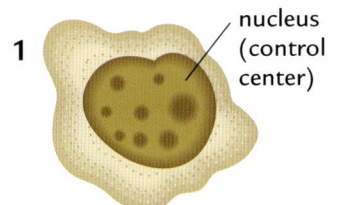 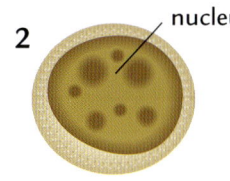 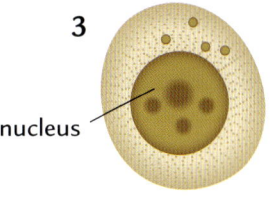 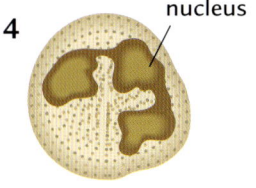

Macrophages (1) engulf and destroy microorganisms. Lymphocytes, T or B cells (2), produce antibodies and kill infected cells. Natural killer cells (3) attack virus-infected or cancerous body cells. Neutrophils (4) destroy bacteria at the site of infection.

which transports oxygen. Around 45 percent of blood consists of red blood cells. They are constantly produced in a tissue called bone marrow in the bones. An adult has around 25 trillion disk-shaped red blood cells in the blood.

White blood cells, also made in the bone marrow, are part of your immune system. They include macrophages, T cells, B cells, natural killer cells, and neutrophils (see 69–70). Platelets are fragments of blood cells that are important in blood clotting. They stick together to form a fine mesh of fibers, which traps more blood cells. This process results in a clot that seals an injury or wound.

▲ White blood cells protect against infection and disease. Each type of cell has a certain job to do. Most white cells in the body are neutrophils.

APPLICATIONS

DONATING BLOOD

Victims of car accidents, people undergoing surgery, and those with certain diseases such as hemophilia (a blood-clotting disorder) often need to receive blood donated by others. Each year about 4 million Americans receive donated blood. A donor's blood is tested to make sure it is healthy. Then about 1 pint (0.5l) of blood is taken from the large vein in the donor's arm. In many cases the donated blood is then separated into its component parts, such as plasma, platelets, and so on. Different patients get just the blood components they need.

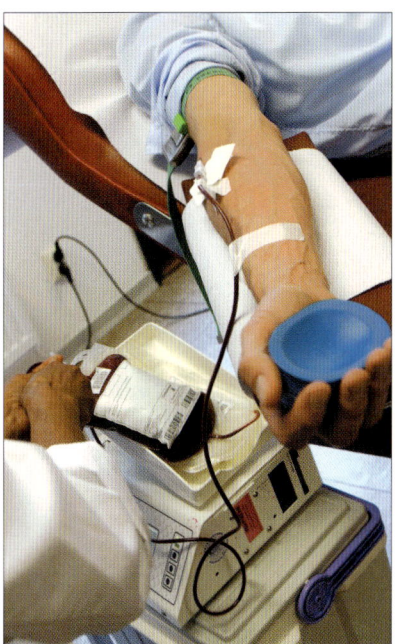

A physician has put a needle into a blood vessel in the donor's arm to take blood.

4 Breathing

Breathing involves the movement of gases between the body and its environment. Biologists call this gas exchange. The organs that carry out this process make up the respiratory system.

Imagine a little girl who does not get what she wants. She may threaten to "hold her breath until she's blue." After one attempt to carry out this threat, most children are smart enough not to try again. But why can't the girl hold her breath for as long as she wants?

Every cell in your body needs a gas called oxygen to function. Breathing helps deliver this gas. It also takes away another gas, carbon

▼ *For people it is impossible to breathe underwater. Divers must use a tank containing oxygen gas as well as other gases to breathe there.*

Breathing

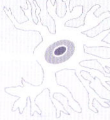

UNDERSTANDING DIFFUSION

Imagine two types of molecules, O and C, separated by a membrane. The concentration of Os is greater on the left, so they diffuse to the right, where there are fewer Os. The concentration of Cs is greater on the right, so they diffuse across the membrane to the left, where there are fewer Cs. In time this diffusion will lead to both sides having equal concentrations of Os and Cs.

dioxide, that is one of the waste products of a cell's functions. The little girl cannot hold her breath until she dies. Breathing is so important that it is controlled by the body's autonomic nervous system. This system regulates crucial body functions automatically in a way that is beyond our conscious control (see 44–55).

Diffusion

Imagine a liquid in a jar separated into two halves by a membrane. One of the halves contains lots of dissolved salt; the other half has just a touch of salt. After a time the salt concentrations in each half will become equal. That is because molecules (small particles) move from places where their concentration is high to places where their concentration is low. This movement of molecules is called diffusion.

Oxygen is needed to break down the fuels such as glucose (see **1**: 28–37) that power cells. As cells use up oxygen, the concentration of oxygen inside becomes lower than the

WATCH DIFFUSION

Use an eyedropper to slowly add a few drops of food coloring to cold water in a clear container, and watch the drops diffuse. Add different colors, and observe the color of the water after 5 minutes and then after 10 minutes. You will see that the colors gradually blend as the food coloring particles diffuse into the water. Eventually the water will become a uniform color.

27

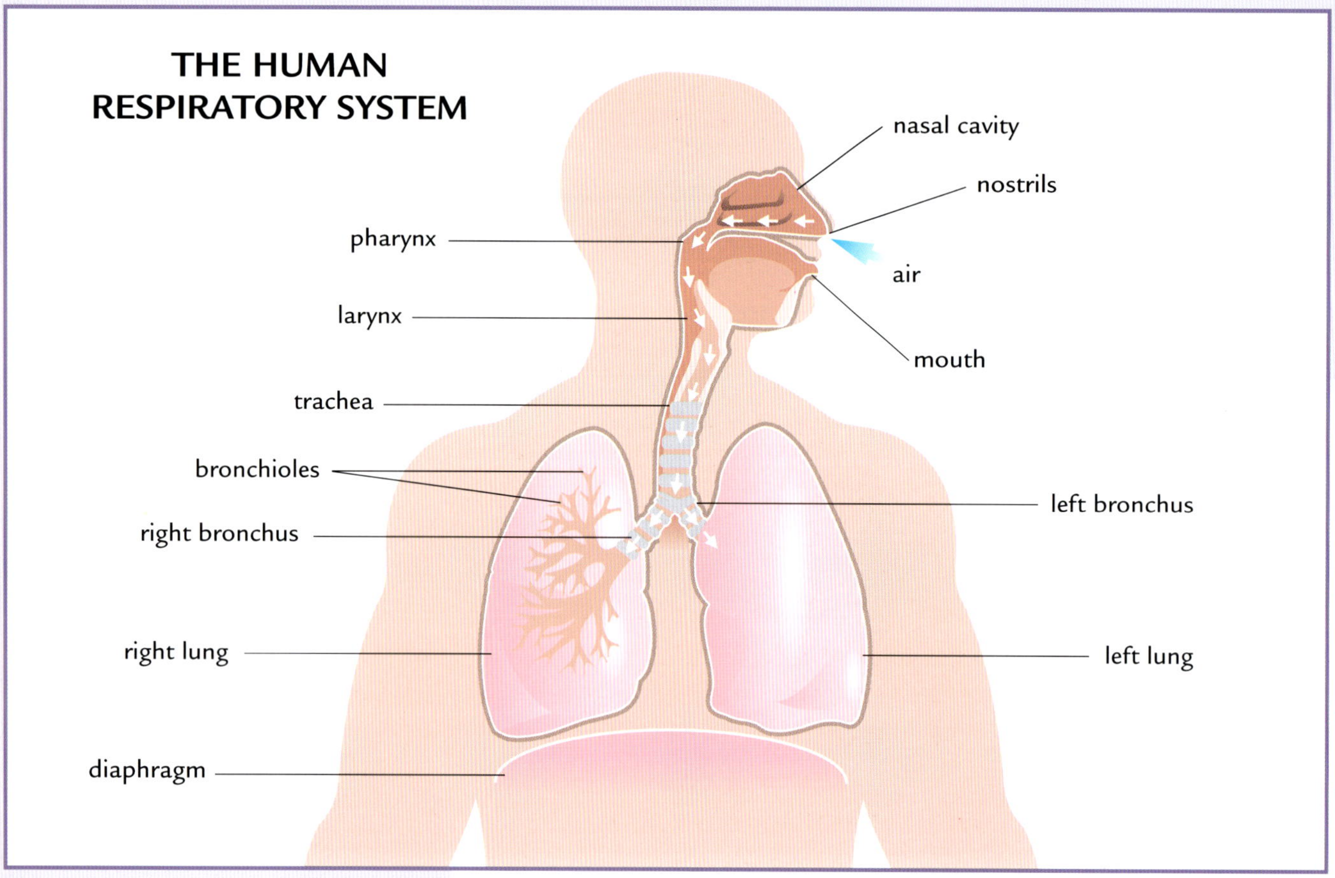

BIOLOGY MATTERS! The Human Body

THE HUMAN RESPIRATORY SYSTEM

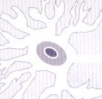

▲ The human respiratory system. The white arrows show the movement of air into the lungs.

concentration outside. So oxygen diffuses in through the cell membrane and into the cell. Similarly, as waste carbon dioxide builds up inside the cell, its concentration becomes higher than outside. Carbon dioxide then diffuses out through the cell membrane.

Diffusion is the key to gas exchange. Large animals with lots of cells, such as people, have respiratory systems in which oxygen and carbon dioxide diffuse in and out of the blood. As it moves through the body, blood comes into contact with body cells. Blood transports gases between the cells and the respiratory organs, the lungs.

The passage of air

Air enters the nose or mouth and goes down a tube called the trachea. It splits into tubelike branches called the bronchi (singular bronchus). The bronchi then enter the lungs, where they branch into even smaller tubes called the bronchioles.

Gas exchange occurs in the lung cells. Lungs contain large numbers of clusters of

Breathing

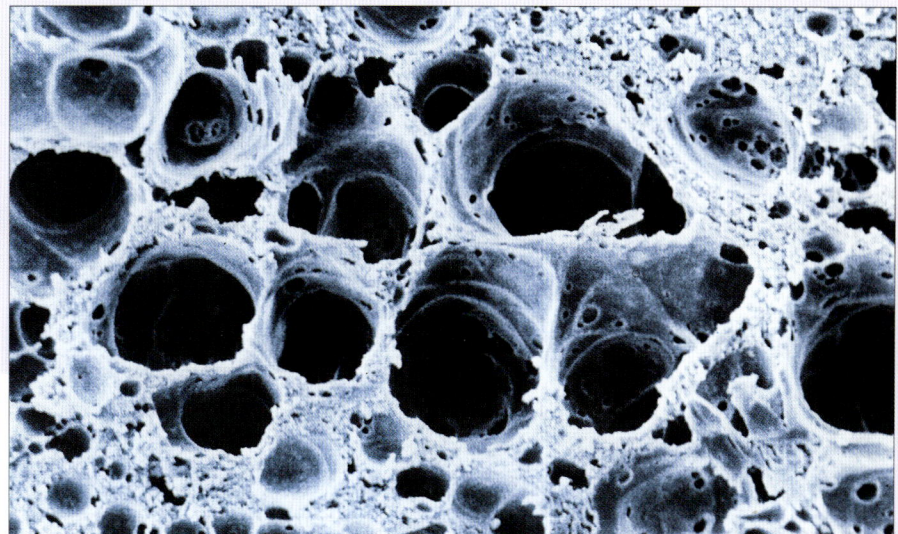

air sacs called alveoli (singular alveolus). The alveoli bunch together like grapes at the tips of the bronchioles. Each bunch is called an alveolar sac. Because each sac contains many alveoli, the surface area available for gas exchange is enormous. The 600 million or so alveoli in a pair of human lungs have a surface area of around 750 square feet (68 square m)—enough to cover a tennis court.

People breathe in oxygen-rich air from the environment and breathe out air laden with carbon dioxide from inside their body. The two gases are constantly being exchanged inside the alveoli. The walls of an alveolus are only one cell thick to help swift diffusion. They are also elastic to allow easy movement of gases in and out of the air sac. Alveoli contain a network of vessels called capillaries that carry blood through the lungs. Gas exchange occurs between the blood in the capillaries and air in the alveoli. Gases move through the moist inner surface of the alveoli.

Blood movements

Blood that enters the lungs from the heart has already made its rounds through

▲ *A section through some alveoli. Their thin walls are just one cell in thickness. Up to 600 million alveoli occur in a person's lungs.*

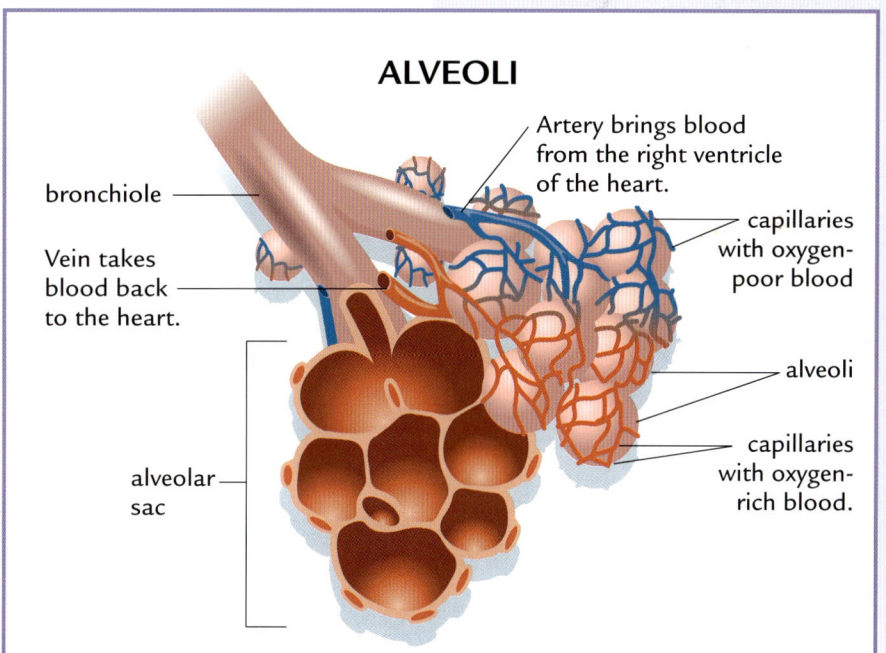

ALVEOLI

- bronchiole
- Vein takes blood back to the heart.
- alveolar sac
- Artery brings blood from the right ventricle of the heart.
- capillaries with oxygen-poor blood
- alveoli
- capillaries with oxygen-rich blood.

BIOLOGY MATTERS! The Human Body

WHAT DO YOU THINK?

SINISTER SMOG

Smog contains substances called pollutants that damage people's health and the environment. They include a gas called ozone, which can make breathing difficult and painful. Smog can be deadly to people suffering from respiratory diseases such as asthma.

Most smog and ozone come from car exhausts. Sport utility vehicles (SUVs) produce the most smog and ozone. But automobile manufacturers have yet to make SUVs more environmentally friendly. Do you think these companies should be forced to build SUVs that produce less pollution? Or should SUV owners pay a "pollution" tax to encourage people to drive less damaging cars?

Smog over Los Angeles is caused by pollutants.

the body, collecting waste products. The concentration of carbon dioxide in this blood is high, while the carbon dioxide concentration in the alveoli is low. So carbon dioxide diffuses out of the blood and into the alveoli. From the alveoli the carbon dioxide leaves the body along the same route that air from outside enters. It is breathed out through the nose and mouth.

The blood that gives up its carbon dioxide is oxygen poor, but it picks up oxygen as it flows through the capillaries surrounding the alveoli. Once the oxygen has diffused into the capillaries, it binds to a molecule called hemoglobin contained inside red blood cells. The oxygen-rich blood then flows from the lungs back to the heart, which pumps it through the rest of the body (see 18–25).

When oxygen-rich blood reaches the body cells, it has a greater concentration of

HOT DEBATE

BREATHING IN FINE PARTICLES

When you breathe in, fine particles 100 times thinner than a human hair from coal-burning power plants may enter your lungs along with oxygen and other gases. These fine particles make breathing problems worse and cause an estimated 150,000 early deaths from lung disease every year. Many people want regulations to limit power-plant emissions, but some think that such regulations will make electricity too expensive.

Breathing

oxygen than they do. So the gas diffuses out of the blood by passing through the capillary membranes and into the cells. At the same time, carbon dioxide from the cells diffuses into the blood. When the blood reenters the lungs, carbon dioxide diffuses through the alveoli and is breathed out of the body.

Cells use oxygen to respire. This involves a chemical reaction between a fuel, such as glucose, and the oxygen to produce energy (2: 30–43).

What is hemoglobin?

Hemoglobin is the substance in red blood cells that binds to and carries oxygen to body cells. Hemoglobin has a chemical "affinity" for oxygen—that is, hemoglobin absorbs many times more oxygen than do other molecules, such as water. In fact, hemoglobin allows blood to carry 70 times more oxygen than it otherwise could. Hemoglobin is essential for efficient oxygen transport.

Looking at lungs

Human lungs are large, triangular organs that are broader at the bottom than at the top.

CLOSEUP: SAVING ENERGY

Moving around costs energy. Animals use a range of strategies to limit energy wasted by breathing while swimming, running, or flying.

For example, when penguins and dolphins swim long distances, they occasionally leap from the water. This behavior is called porpoising. Porpoising does not help these animals travel faster, but it does allow them to breathe while maintaining their speed. Another neat trick is used by animals such as kangaroos, horses, and dogs. Biologists have found that these beasts take one breath per step as they run or hop. At speed they use the motion of organs inside them such as the liver to breathe. The movement shifts the diaphragm (see 34). That allows the animal to breathe without wasting energy on muscular movements of the ribs and diaphragm, as people must do.

Kangaroos (left) "vibrate" to breathe when they hop quickly. The motion of their internal organs moves the diaphragm, helping them save energy.

BIOLOGY MATTERS! The Human Body

WHAT DO YOU THINK?

CIGARETTES AND BREATHING

Smoking cigarettes and other tobacco products damages the lungs and causes fatal diseases. Antismoking regulations are becoming more common and widespread. In many places smoking is now banned in public places, such as bars, restaurants, and sports stadiums.

Second-hand cigarette smoke breathed out by smokers may harm people nearby. This is called passive smoking. Yet most smokers claim they have a right to smoke cigarettes, especially in outside places where the smoke can disperse in the air.

Do you think that there is a point at which antismoking laws interfere with a citizen's right to smoke if he or she wants to? Or do you think that something that could damage other people's health should be banned outright?

They are enclosed in two baglike membranes called pleurae (sing. pleura). The inner pleura attaches to the spongy tissue of the lungs. The outer pleura is a stronger, tougher protective membrane. The lungs are protected further by the rib cage (see 34–43), which surrounds them.

How do people breathe?
At the base of the lungs lies the diaphragm, a strong, elastic muscle that controls breathing. The diaphragm forms a partition between the

APPLICATIONS

VENTILATORS

A mechanical ventilator is a machine that "breathes" for someone with breathing problems. A ventilator monitors the flow of gases in and out of the patient. Oxygen flows from a container, through tubes, and into the patient's lungs. The machine controls the exact amount and pressure. It regulates the airflow carefully, so the lungs are not expanded too much or too little, and the alveoli are not damaged. The rate of breathing is also controlled, so breathing in and out occurs at normal intervals.

chest and the abdomen. When relaxed, the diaphragm is domed and curves upward to rest in the chest. When the diaphragm contracts, it flattens and moves lower, increasing the volume of the rib cage, which sucks air into the lungs. The contraction of the muscles between the ribs causes the rib cage to lift and move out, increasing the volume of the lungs and also causing air to enter them from the bronchi.

When the diaphragm and rib cage muscles relax, the ribs move back, down, and in. The volume of the lungs decreases, and air is forced out of the body. The person then breathes out. The diaphragm resumes its domed position inside the

TRY THIS

DIFFICULT BREATHING

Some lung diseases—such as an illness called emphysema caused by smoking—destroy lung tissue or make the alveoli unable to absorb oxygen.

To get an idea of the effects of destroyed lung tissue, get a drinking straw, and put one end between your lips (right). Close your lips tightly around the straw. For one full minute breathe in and out only through the straw. This will give you some idea how it feels to have a lung disease such as emphysema.

BREATHING IN AND OUT

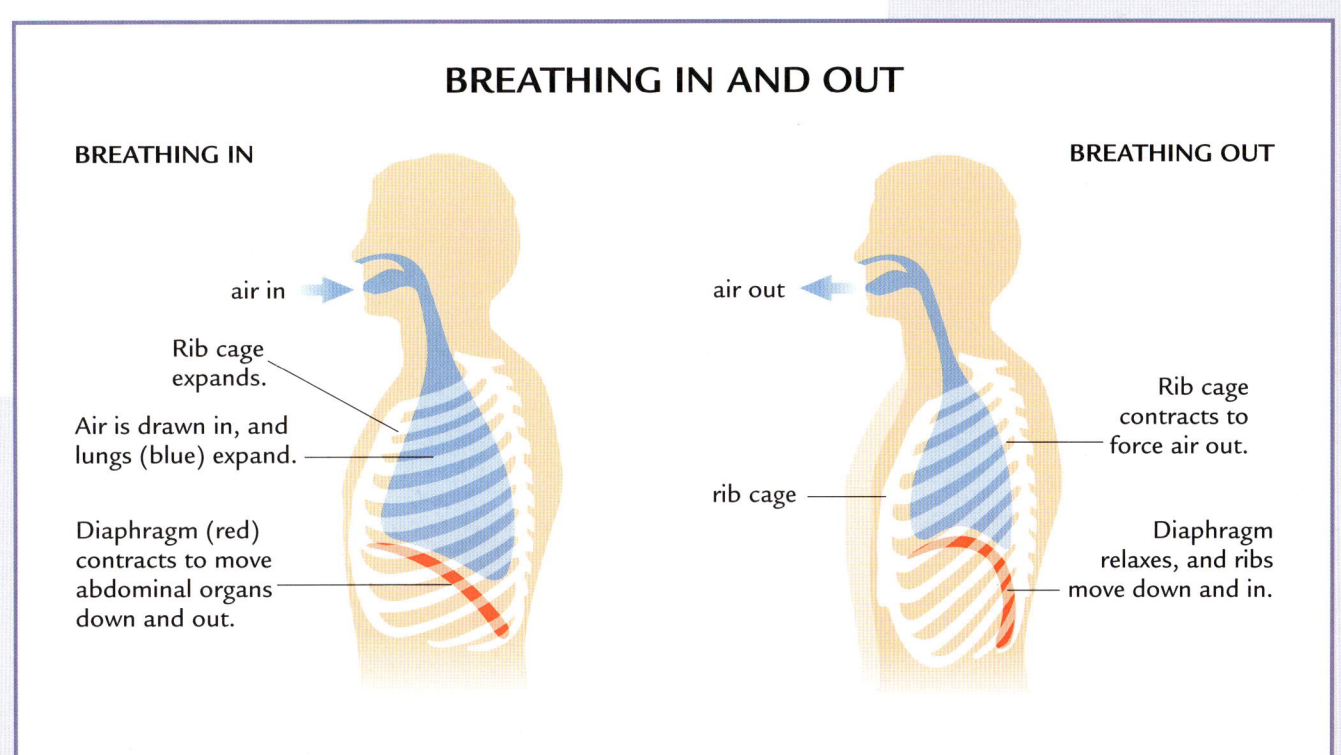

BREATHING IN
- air in
- Rib cage expands.
- Air is drawn in, and lungs (blue) expand.
- Diaphragm (red) contracts to move abdominal organs down and out.

BREATHING OUT
- air out
- Rib cage contracts to force air out.
- rib cage
- Diaphragm relaxes, and ribs move down and in.

5 Muscles and Bones

The bones form a framework for the body called the skeleton. Muscles are bundles of fibers that are attached to the bones. The muscles and bones work together to allow you to move.

The main functions of the skeleton are to provide support to the body, to anchor attached muscles and thus allow movement, to protect vital internal organs, and to create a constant supply of blood cells.

THE SKELETON

Your skeleton has two main parts. One is called the axial skeleton, which includes the cranium (skull), the vertebral column (backbone), and the rib cage. The other is called the appendicular skeleton, which includes the bones of the limbs, the hips, and the shoulders.

An animal's appendicular skeleton determines how it moves—for example, whether it walks on two or four legs, runs, swims, or flies.

Bones meet at joints, of which there are several kinds. Different joints allow the bones to move in different

▼ Arm wrestlers try to outcompete each other. They are using their arm muscles and bones to prove who is the strongest.

Muscles and Bones

directions. Some joints, such as most in your skull, permit no movement at all. You might have muscles that allow you to wiggle your ears, but there is no way you can flex your skull.

Bone
The human skeleton is made of a hard tissue called bone. Although bones vary in size and shape, they all have a similar structure. Bone consists mainly of inorganic

▼ Major bones of the human body. Our 206 bones include 22 in the skull and, although skull bones are fused together in adults, they are still counted as 22 separate bones.

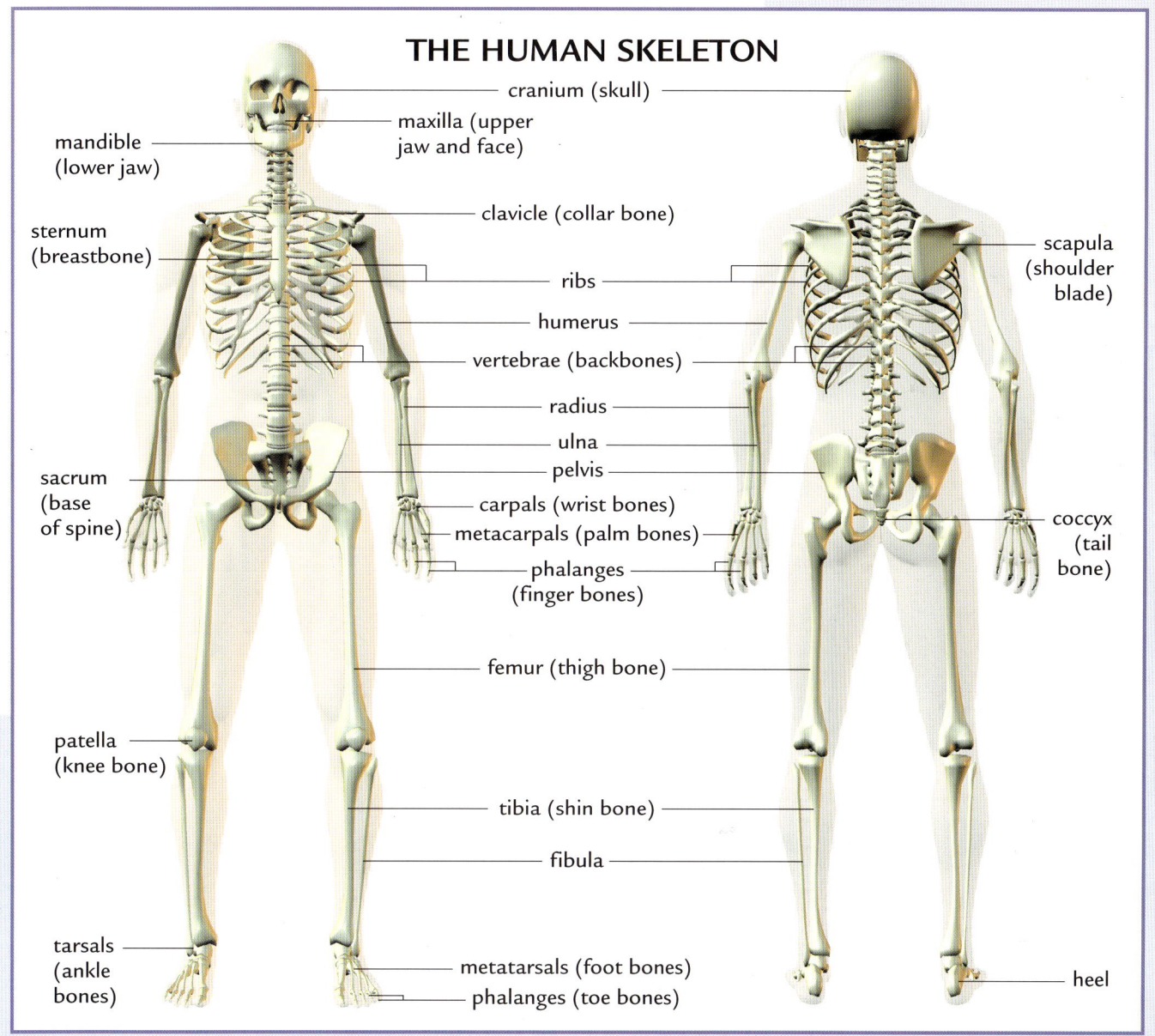

THE HUMAN SKELETON
- cranium (skull)
- maxilla (upper jaw and face)
- mandible (lower jaw)
- clavicle (collar bone)
- sternum (breastbone)
- scapula (shoulder blade)
- ribs
- humerus
- vertebrae (backbones)
- radius
- ulna
- pelvis
- sacrum (base of spine)
- carpals (wrist bones)
- metacarpals (palm bones)
- coccyx (tail bone)
- phalanges (finger bones)
- femur (thigh bone)
- patella (knee bone)
- tibia (shin bone)
- fibula
- tarsals (ankle bones)
- metatarsals (foot bones)
- phalanges (toe bones)
- heel

BIOLOGY MATTERS! The Human Body

CLOSEUP

EXOSKELETONS

Many invertebrates (animals without backbones) such as insects and crabs have an exoskeleton. It is a hard casing on the outside of the body. The exoskeleton serves three major functions—it protects the body, serves as an attachment point for muscles, and helps reduce water loss.

Exoskeletons cannot usually expand, though. In order to grow, the animal makes a new exoskeleton under the old one. The old skin is then shed in a process called molting. The animal quickly expands while the new exoskeleton is soft. This can be a dangerous time for the temporarily unprotected animal. It must wait for the new exoskeleton to harden before it regains its protective covering.

materials, such as calcium and phosphorus, and protein fibers called collagen. Inorganic materials are those that do not contain carbon. Calcium and phosphorus give bone its strength and hardness. Collagen fibers give bone its flexibility. Bone cells, called osteocytes, are embedded in a mass of minerals and collagen fibers. Osteocytes are living cells, and they are surrounded by a network of tiny blood vessels called capillaries (see 23–24).

Most bone has three layers. The outer, protective layer is called the periosteum. It is the layer from which new bone forms. The periosteum is riddled with blood vessels and nerve endings. When you break a bone, the pain you feel comes from nerves in the periosteum.

Beneath the periosteum lies the white, rock-hard compact bone that supports the body's weight. Compact bone contains a network of tiny chambers, each of which contains an osteocyte.

The innermost and least dense layer of bone is called spongy bone, or bone marrow. This layer is where blood cells are produced. Spongy bone contains two types of marrow.

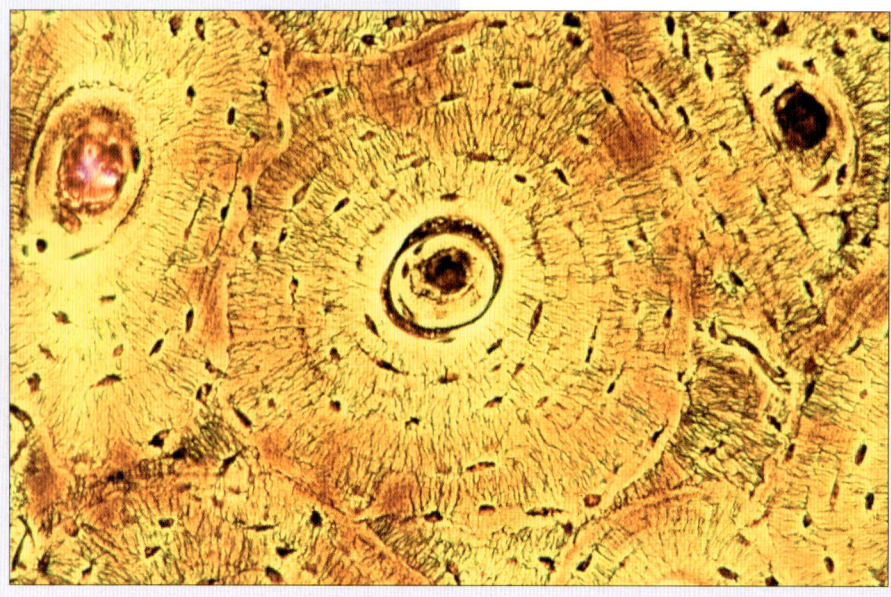

◀ A cross section through compact bone. Bone has a distinctive appearance—like layers of circles or tree rings. The small dark ovals are osteocytes (a type of bone cell).

Red marrow produces blood cells (see 25), while yellow marrow stores fat.

Bone growth

Bone is constantly being broken down and rebuilt. Three types of bone cells are involved in this process. Osteoclasts break down and dissolve old and damaged bones. Osteoblasts make new bone tissue. Osteocytes maintain the right amount of calcium and phosphorus in newly created bone.

Leg and arm bones grow, or elongate (get longer), from sites called growth plates. They are near the ends of the bones. A white, flexible tissue called cartilage occurs at the growth plates. Connective tissue forms around the cartilage, eventually turning it into compact bone. Blood vessels extend from the bone marrow into the developing bone. Bone formation continues throughout childhood. When

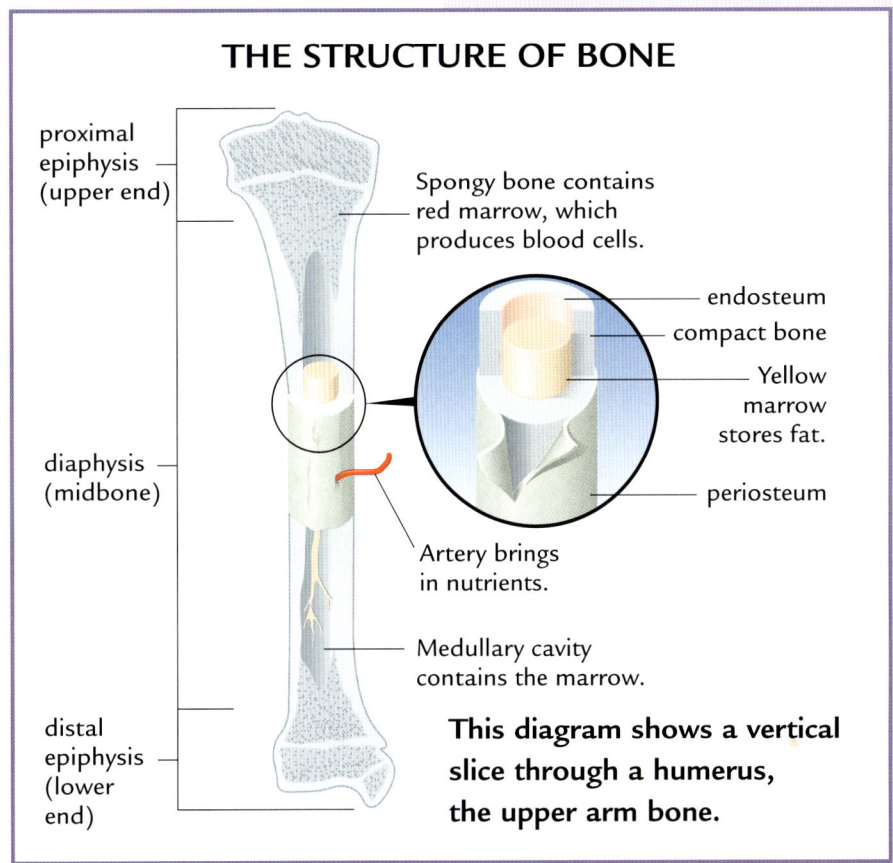

THE STRUCTURE OF BONE

This diagram shows a vertical slice through a humerus, the upper arm bone.

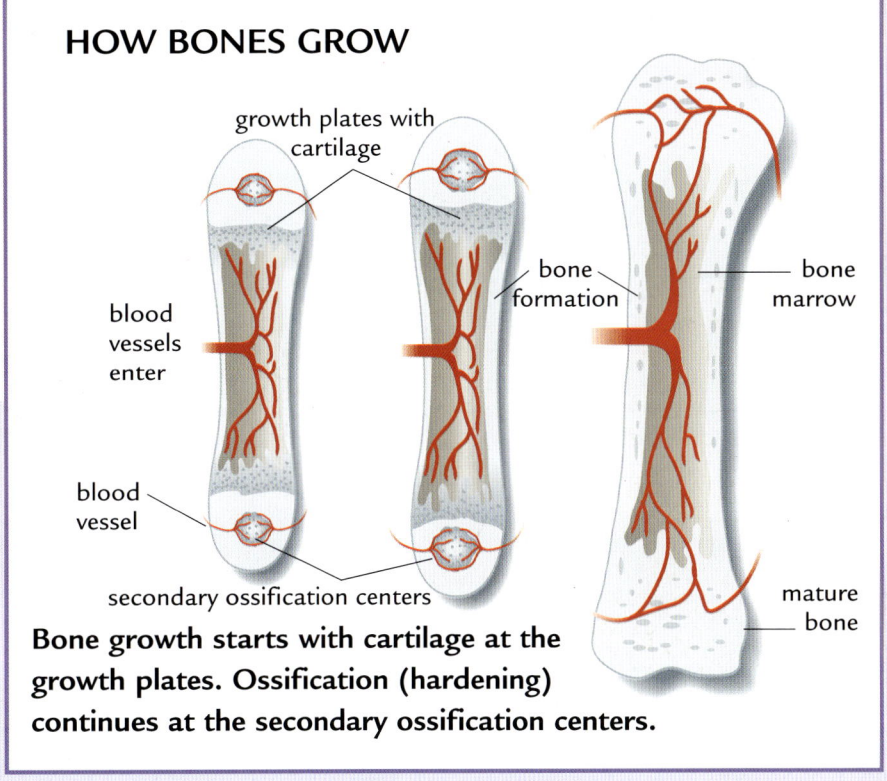

HOW BONES GROW

Bone growth starts with cartilage at the growth plates. Ossification (hardening) continues at the secondary ossification centers.

BIOLOGY MATTERS! The Human Body

OSTEOPOROSIS

One out of two women and one out of eight men experience bone loss as they get older. This condition is called osteoporosis. It can arise as a result of lack of exercise, a calcium-poor diet, or the hormonal changes that occur during and after menopause (when menstruation stops). Some doctors state that osteoporosis can be prevented if children and young adults keep up a lifelong routine of regular exercise and eat a diet rich in calcium or take calcium supplements to prevent bone loss later in life. How would you alter your diet and daily life to help prevent osteoporosis when you grow older?

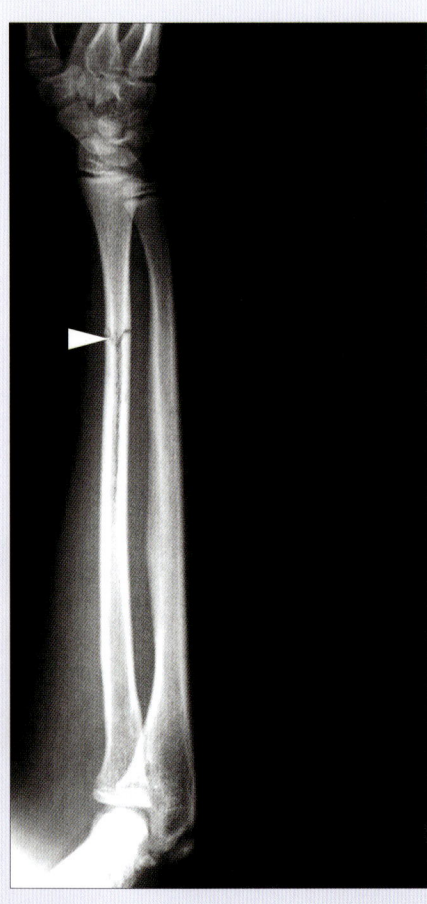

▲ An X-ray showing a simple fracture of the arm. Casts of plaster are used to hold the two broken bone ends in place so they can knit together correctly.

you reach your full height and your bones are fully shaped, bone elongation stops. Although adult bones do not elongate, they can be strengthened by exercise.

The axial skeleton

Your skull contains 29 bones, but most of them (especially those at the top) are fused together. The skull is made of thick, hard bone and protects the body's control center—the brain. The only bones in the skull that move are the jaw and the tiny bones of the middle ear. The jaw is hinged to the skull and can move up and down and, to a lesser extent, sideways. This movable jaw enables people to eat and to communicate with each other.

The backbone, or vertebral column, protects the spinal cord, which is made up of nerves carrying vital messages to and from the brain. The backbone is made up of a series of 33 bones called vertebrae (singular vertebra). The backbone permits a degree of movement, allowing you to bend and twist. The spinal cord enters the brain at an opening in the base of the skull. The skull and the backbone meet at a joint that allows the head to move up and down and side to side.

The rib cage consists of the sternum and 12 pairs of ribs. Each pair of ribs is attached to one of the vertebrae in the backbone. The sternum consists of three bones that together are also called the breastbone.

The appendicular skeleton

The appendicular skeleton consists of the pelvic girdle (hip bones) and leg bones, the

Muscles and Bones

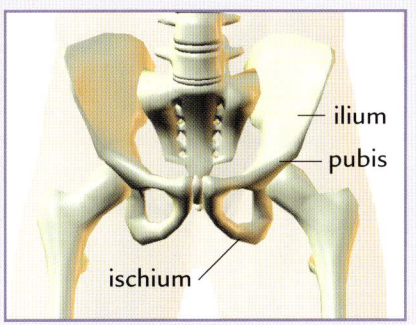

◀ The pelvic girdle. The hip bones actually consist of three bones. They are fused to provide strength and support for the organs inside.

▶ The pectoral girdle consists of the scapulae and clavicles.

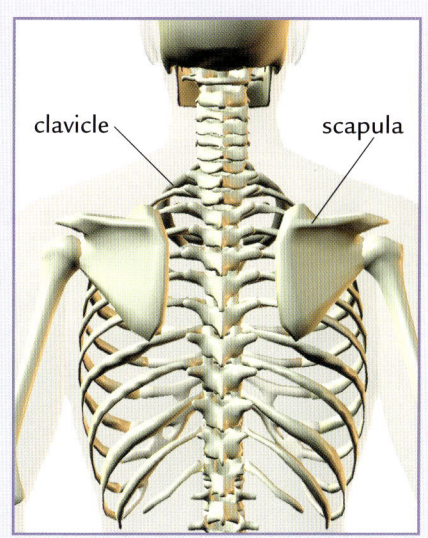

pectoral girdle (shoulder blades and collar bones), and arm bones. The bones in the pelvic girdle allow limited movement. There are six pairs of mostly fused bones, plus some of the lower vertebrae, in the adult pelvic girdle. The pelvic bones are fused to help strengthen the pelvic girdle. This provides more protection for the pelvic organs.

The femur (thighbone) meets the pelvic girdle at the hip socket. This joint is formed by three fused pelvic bones. Going down the leg, the femur is connected to the knee bone, then to the shin bones (tibia and fibula) and then to the bones of the ankle and foot.

Your body's other girdle—the pectoral girdle—consists of your two shoulder blades (called scapulae) and two collar bones (called clavicles). The scapulae (singular scapula) are flat, thick bones ideal for the attachment of strong arm muscles. The clavicles meet the scapulae on the front side of the shoulder joint. The clavicles join in the middle of the sternum. Also joined to the scapulae are the upper arm bone (humerus), the bones of the forearm (radius and ulna), and the bones of the wrist and hand.

Joints

Most bones meet at joints—connections that allow the bones to move a certain amount in one or more directions. There are three types of joints: immovable, partly movable, and synovial joints.

Immovable joints consist of fused bones, as in the skull. Partly movable joints like those between the vertebrae often have cartilage between them and are flexible in limited directions. Synovial joints, such as those of the shoulders, allow for a wider range of movement. Joints prevent the grinding of bone against bone when you move.

APPLICATIONS

ARTIFICIAL BONES AND JOINTS

When they are injured or diseased, entire bones or joints sometimes need to be replaced. Surgeons remove the old joint or bone (often a hip or knee) and implant a new one. In the 1920s implants were made of stainless steel. By the 1950s manufacturers of implants used pure titanium, another metal. Both materials were problematic. Body fluids damaged them, and they were not very strong or long lasting. The latest implants are made of a combination of the metals nickel and titanium called nitinol. Nitinol is not eroded by the body, and it is strong and flexible.

BIOLOGY MATTERS! The Human Body

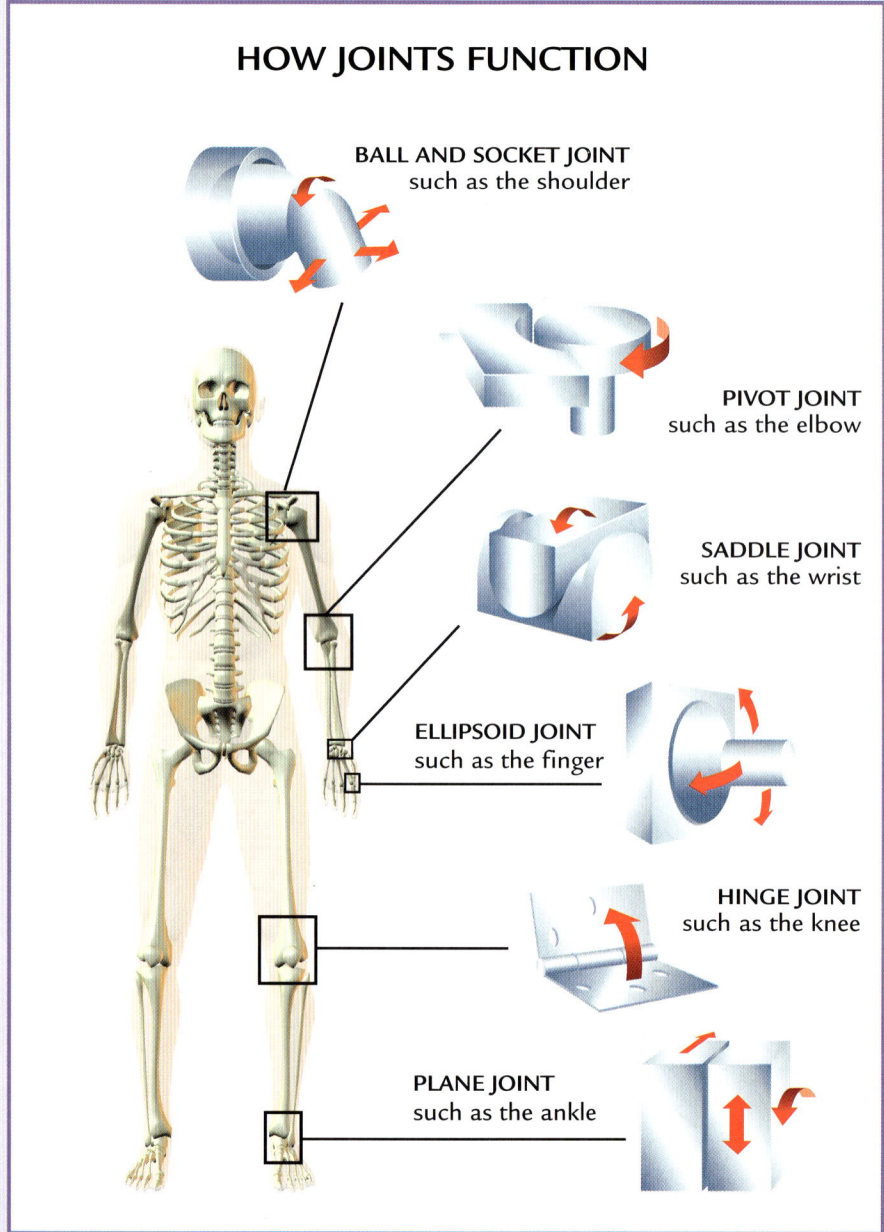

HOW JOINTS FUNCTION

BALL AND SOCKET JOINT such as the shoulder

PIVOT JOINT such as the elbow

SADDLE JOINT such as the wrist

ELLIPSOID JOINT such as the finger

HINGE JOINT such as the knee

PLANE JOINT such as the ankle

Where two bones meet at a joint, there are extremely smooth layers of cartilage. Synovial joints also produce a lubricant (slippery substance) called synovial fluid. The fluid serves to lubricate all parts of the joint. Bones that meet at a joint are held together by tough ligaments. Ligaments are a type of tough connective tissue. When people damage a ligament, they are said to have a "sprain."

MUSCLES

Muscles are bundles of fibers most of which are attached to and pull on your bones. In this way they move your body. They can do so because muscle cells are master shape shifters. They change their shape by squeezing (contracting); they never push.

◀ *Different joints in the body allow different degrees of freedom, as shown by the arrows in this diagram.*

APPLICATIONS

BIOFEEDBACK

Biofeedback is a technique in which you learn how to control body processes that you cannot normally consciously affect. You are connected to an electronic monitoring machine via electrodes (electric sensors) taped to your body. A monitor shows your blood pressure, heartbeat, temperature, and brain activity. A biofeedback expert teaches you how to relax your muscles and control your breathing as you watch

Muscles and Bones

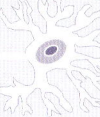

 **APPLICATIONS**

SMART PROSTHESES

A prosthesis is an artificial body part, such as an arm or a leg. Wooden legs replace limbs but do not work as well as the original. Some modern prostheses, however, behave more like living limbs and respond to electrical impulses the way muscles do. The prostheses are controlled by sophisticated electronics in contact with the user's own muscle and with sensors in the prosthesis. The sensors detect tiny electrical signals in the human muscle and transmit the signal to the artificial limb. This artificial limb is powered by batteries and moves the prosthesis in a way similar to natural limb movement.

There are three basic types of muscles—smooth muscle, skeletal muscle, and cardiac muscle. Smooth muscles line most of your internal organs, such as your stomach, intestines, and blood vessels. These muscles move without you willing them to because they are controlled by the autonomic nervous system (see 44–46).

Skeletal muscles attach to the bones that they move. They are also called voluntary muscles (because they are under your control most of the time) or striated muscles

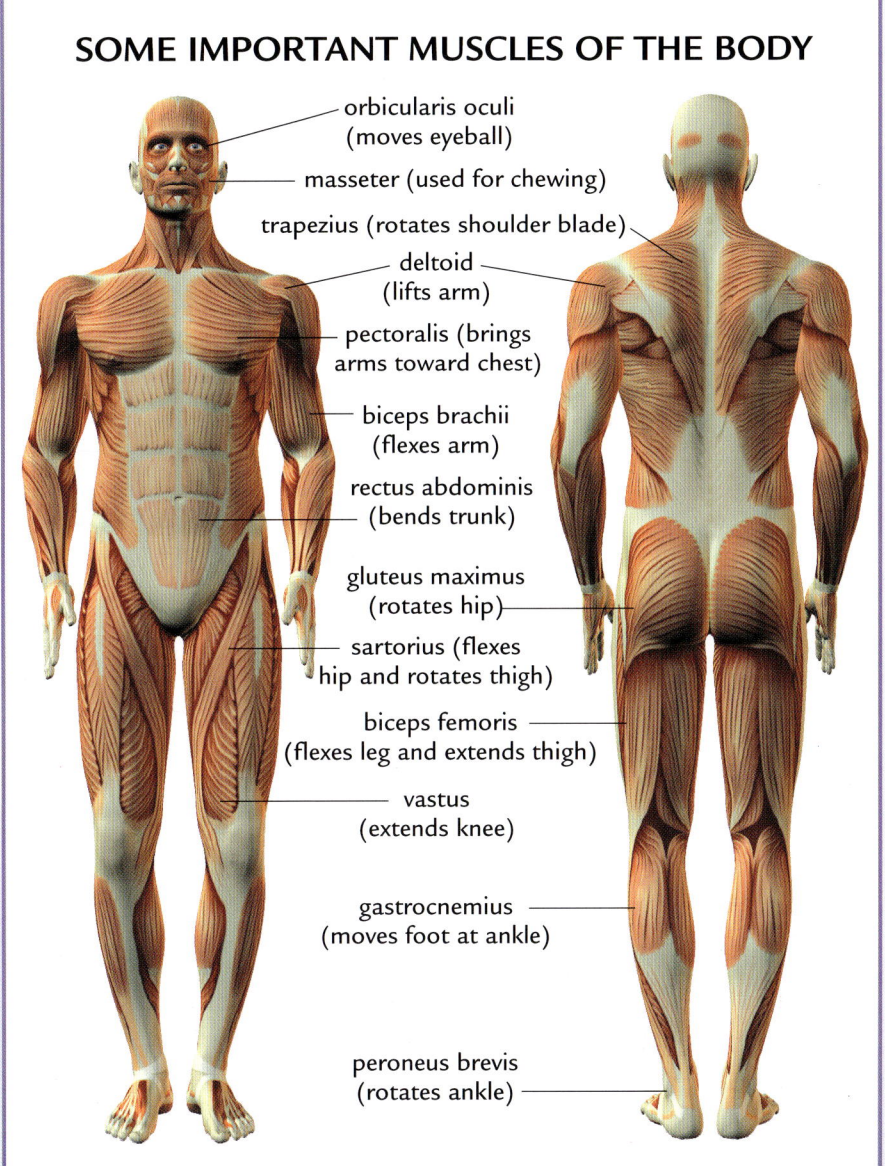

SOME IMPORTANT MUSCLES OF THE BODY

- orbicularis oculi (moves eyeball)
- masseter (used for chewing)
- trapezius (rotates shoulder blade)
- deltoid (lifts arm)
- pectoralis (brings arms toward chest)
- biceps brachii (flexes arm)
- rectus abdominis (bends trunk)
- gluteus maximus (rotates hip)
- sartorius (flexes hip and rotates thigh)
- biceps femoris (flexes leg and extends thigh)
- vastus (extends knee)
- gastrocnemius (moves foot at ankle)
- peroneus brevis (rotates ankle)

the effects on the monitor. In time you learn to use these relaxation techniques without the monitor. This lowers your blood pressure.

BIOLOGY MATTERS! The Human Body

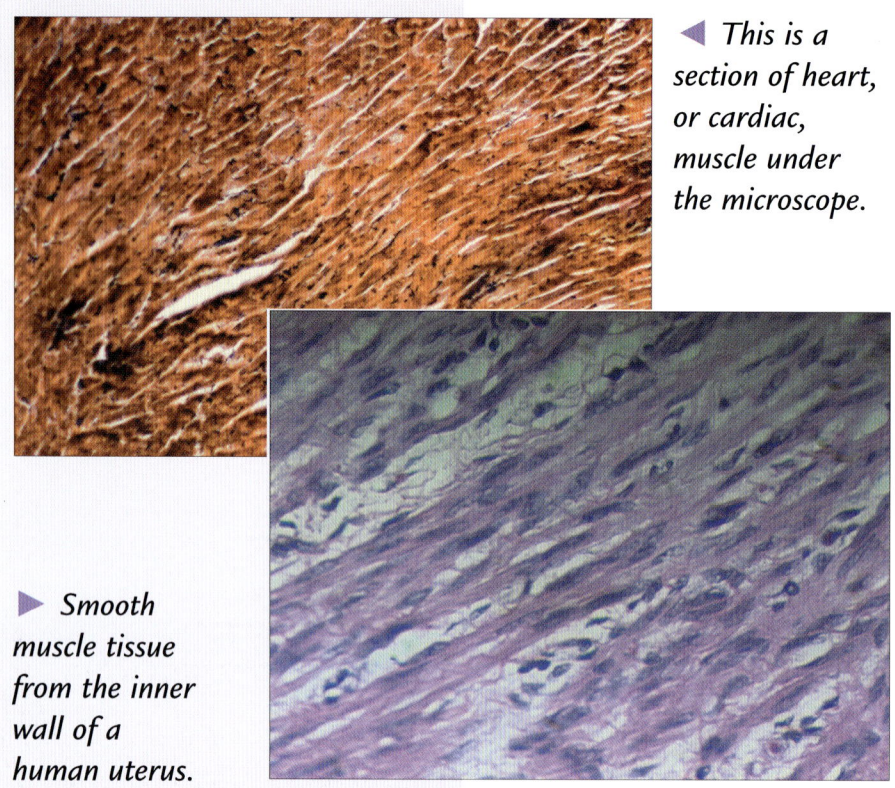

◀ This is a section of heart, or cardiac, muscle under the microscope.

▶ Smooth muscle tissue from the inner wall of a human uterus.

(because under a microscope they look striated, or striped). Cardiac (heart) muscles are involuntary muscles, but the heart has its own system of internal controls (see 19–21). The muscles of the heart are unique in that they have characteristics of both smooth muscles and skeletal muscles.

Most muscles are attached directly to the bones in your skeleton. Many of your lip and face muscles, however, are not attached directly to bone. All skeletal muscles have lots of sensory nerves (see 44–55) that tell the brain what a muscle is doing.

Skeletal muscle cells are also called muscle fibers. Muscle fibers are strongly bound in a bundle called a fasicle. Fasicles are tied together and covered by a strong casing of connective tissue called the fascia. At the ends of a muscle the fascia bind together to form a dense collagen tissue called a tendon. Tendons attach at one end to voluntary muscle and at the other to the bone that the muscle moves.

MUSCLE ANTAGONISM

Muscles often work in tandem to get a job done. This is called muscle antagonism. The muscles work around a pivot point, or fulcrum. The pull of one muscle (effort) is opposed by resistance from another (load).

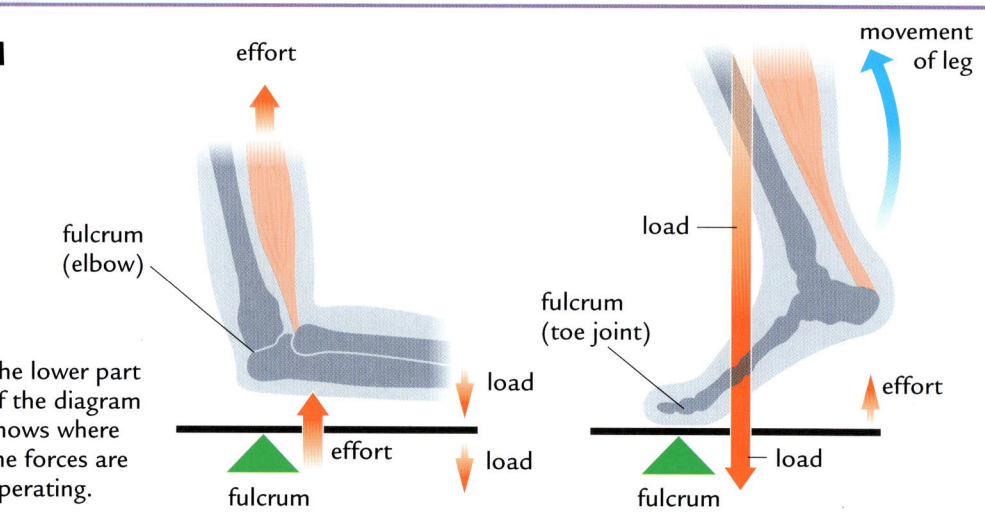

The lower part of the diagram shows where the forces are operating.

Muscles and Bones

Muscle antagonism

Most skeletal muscles work by opposing the actions of other muscles. Thus, when one muscle contracts, its opposite (the antagonist muscle) relaxes and is stretched (see below). For example, when you lift something with your arm, nerve signals from the brain travel to your arm muscles and tell the muscles on the front of your upper arm—the biceps—to contract, or flex. At the same time, the opposing muscle to the biceps on the back of your arm—the triceps—relaxes and extends to allow your arm to bend. In this example the muscle that contracts is called the flexor muscle, and the muscle that relaxes is called the extensor muscle. If, while you are contracting one muscle, you do not let its antagonist muscle relax, the muscles simply bulge.

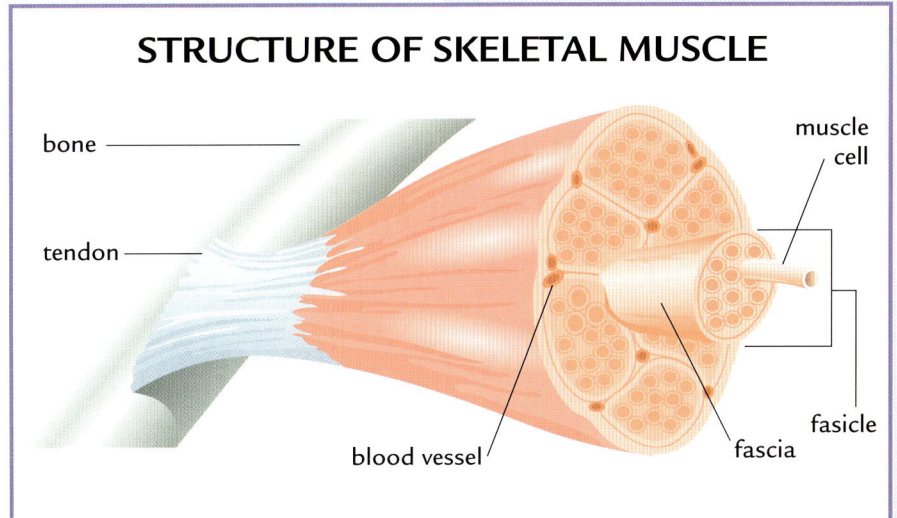

Muscle contraction

Muscles contract when they receive electrical signals from the brain and other parts of the central nervous system (see 44–55). The signals travel from the brain along nerves called motor neurons (see 46), a type of nerve cell, that lead from the spinal cord to muscles. The neurons release a chemical that makes the muscle contract.

HOT DEBATE: STEROIDS

Some athletes and bodybuilders take artificial chemicals, called anabolic steroids, to improve the size and strength of their muscles. Anabolic steroids are related to naturally occurring chemicals called hormones that are present in the body.

Using anabolic steroids that have not been prescribed by a doctor is illegal and very dangerous. Yet the pressure to excel at sports or to look big and strong tempts some people to abuse anabolic steroids. Despite their side effects (acne, liver damage, and aggression), some athletes feel they must take steroids to compete.

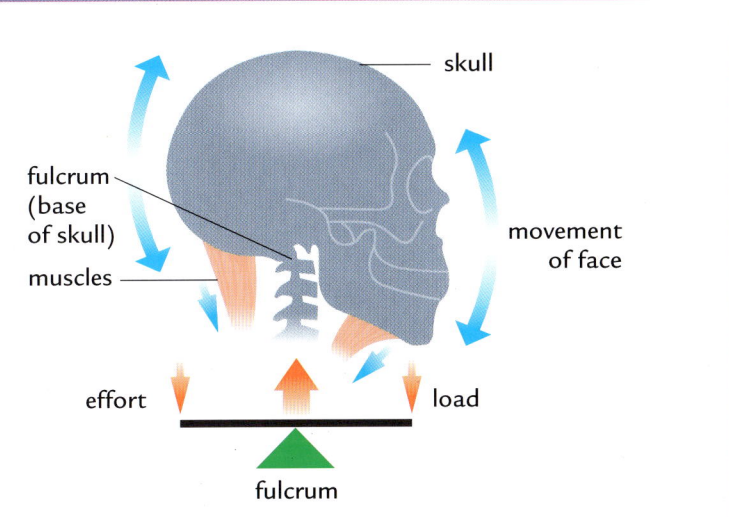

6 The Nervous System

Your nervous system is a huge network of 100 billion nerve cells. It coordinates how you react to events that take place around you.

The nervous system senses the outside world and helps you react to events there by thinking, moving, and speaking. It also regulates many functions inside your body, such as breathing (see 26–33) and heart rate (see 18–25). Nerves contain bundles of thousands of nerve cells, or neurons. They transmit messages in the form of electrical signals that travel along their length (see 48).

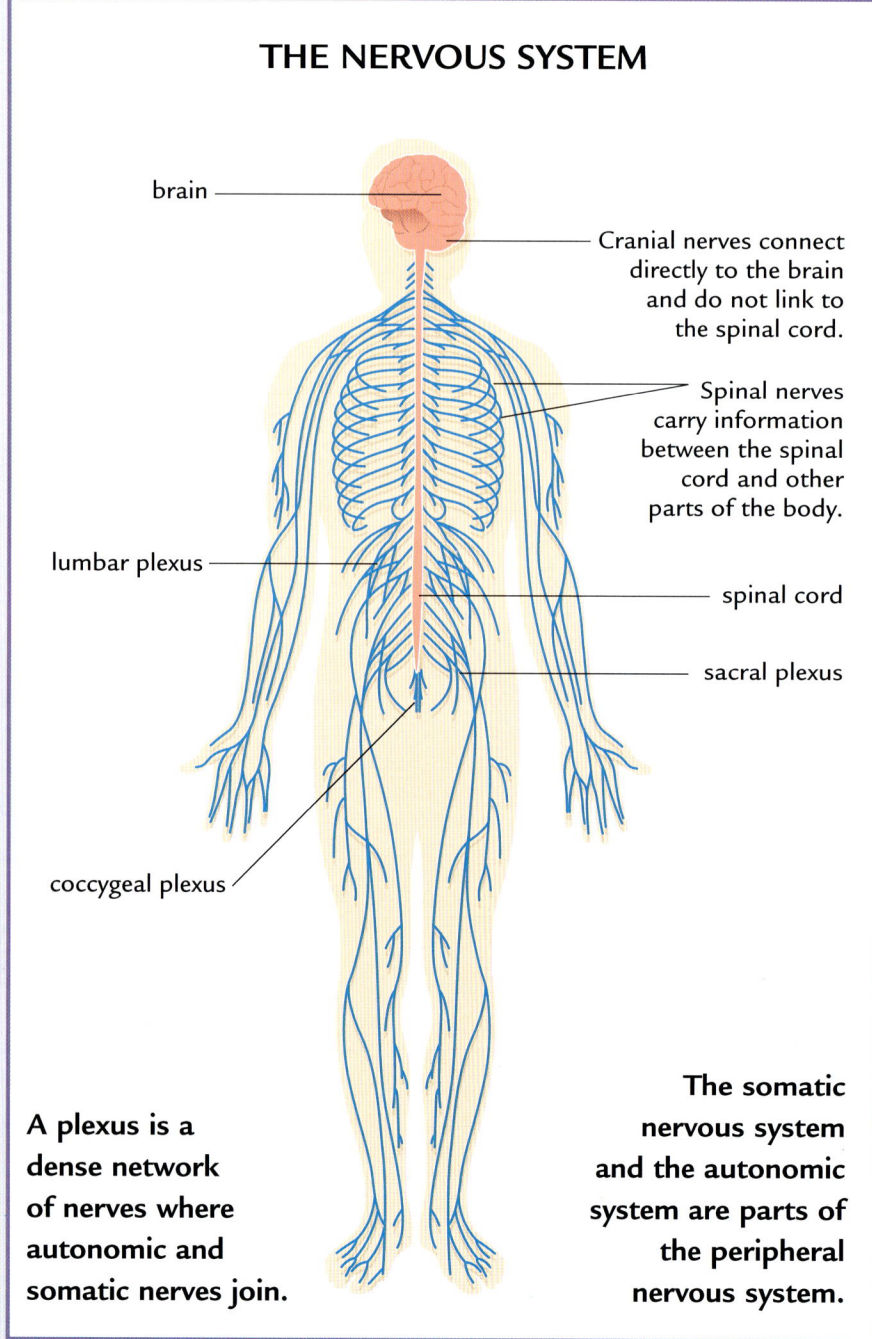

THE NERVOUS SYSTEM

- brain
- Cranial nerves connect directly to the brain and do not link to the spinal cord.
- Spinal nerves carry information between the spinal cord and other parts of the body.
- lumbar plexus
- spinal cord
- sacral plexus
- coccygeal plexus

A plexus is a dense network of nerves where autonomic and somatic nerves join.

The somatic nervous system and the autonomic system are parts of the peripheral nervous system.

◀ The central nervous system (CNS) is shown in red; the peripheral nervous system (PNS) is shown in blue.

The Nervous System

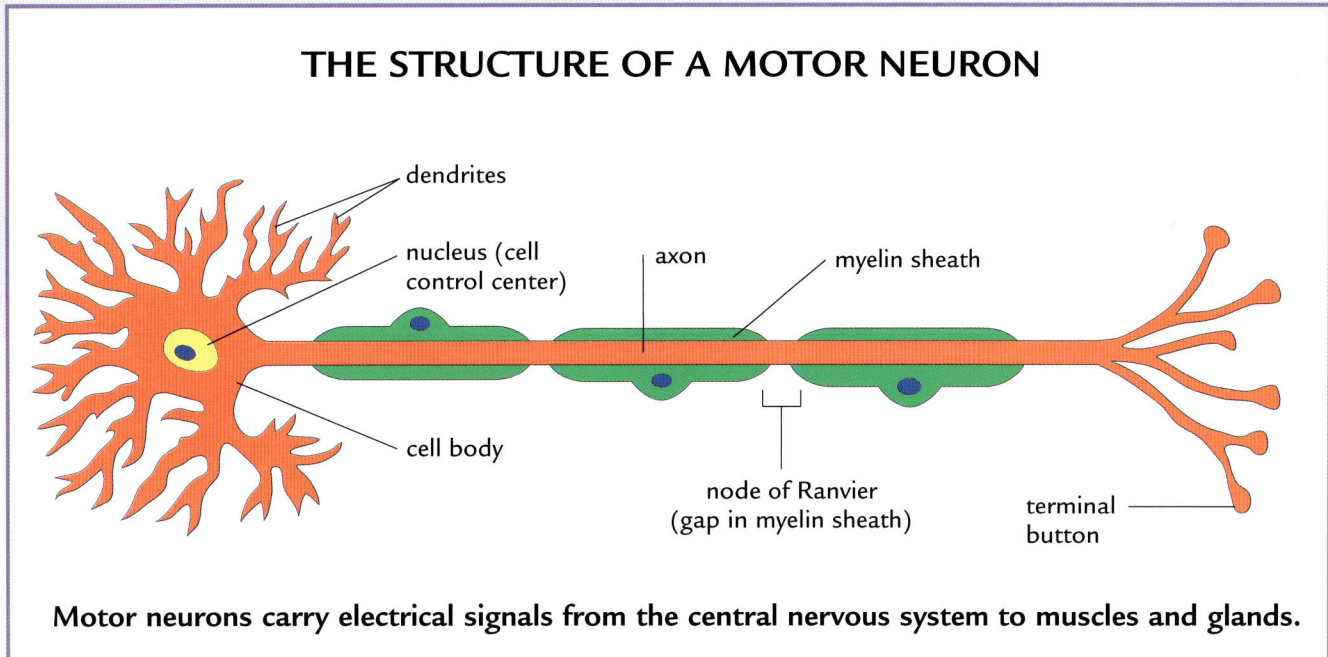

THE STRUCTURE OF A MOTOR NEURON

Motor neurons carry electrical signals from the central nervous system to muscles and glands.

Your nervous system has two main parts. They are called the central nervous system and the peripheral nervous system. The central nervous system, or CNS, is made up of the brain and a collection of nerve cells called the spinal cord that run along the back to the brain. The CNS also contains cells called glia that nourish and protect the neurons.

The CNS acts as the body's control and processing unit. The peripheral nervous system, or PNS, is different. It consists of a network of nerves that spread from the central nervous system to other parts of the body. The PNS has two main parts, the somatic nervous system and the autonomic nervous

▲ Motor neurons are nerve cells that carry signals from the brain to organs, tissues, and glands. Each has a cell body, a long extension called an axon, and shorter extensions called dendrites.

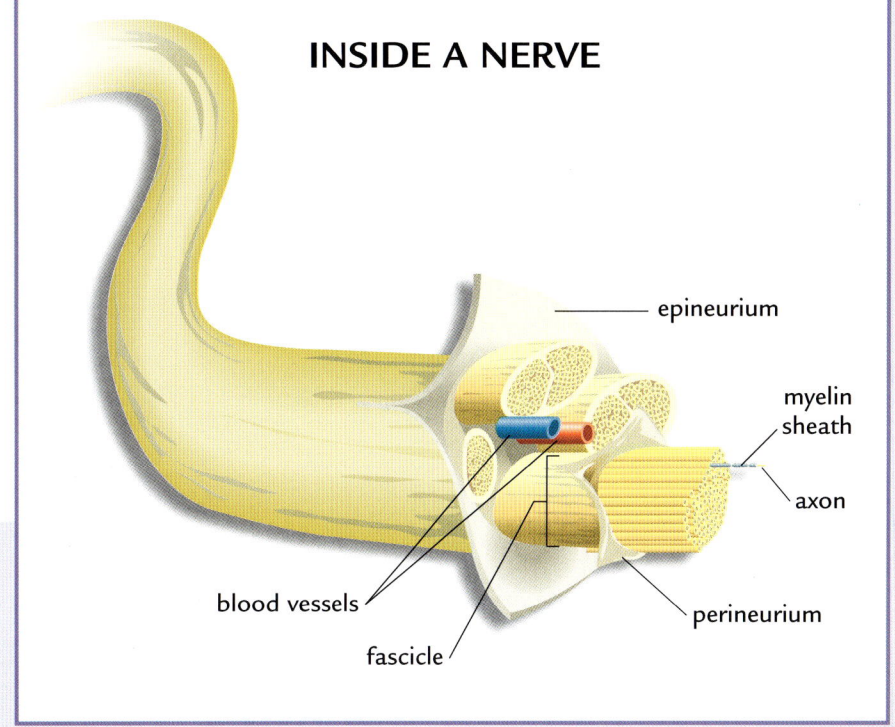

INSIDE A NERVE

▶ A nerve contains many axons, each wrapped by a myelin sheath. The axons are grouped into fasicles.

BIOLOGY MATTERS! The Human Body

RUBBING TO REDUCE PAIN

Have you ever wondered why, when you stub your toe or bang your elbow, rubbing the injured area extremely vigorously can limit the pain a little? Rubbing like this stimulates vast numbers of sensory receptors. They send a barrage of signals to the brain. The jumble of signals makes it difficult for your brain to perceive the pain.

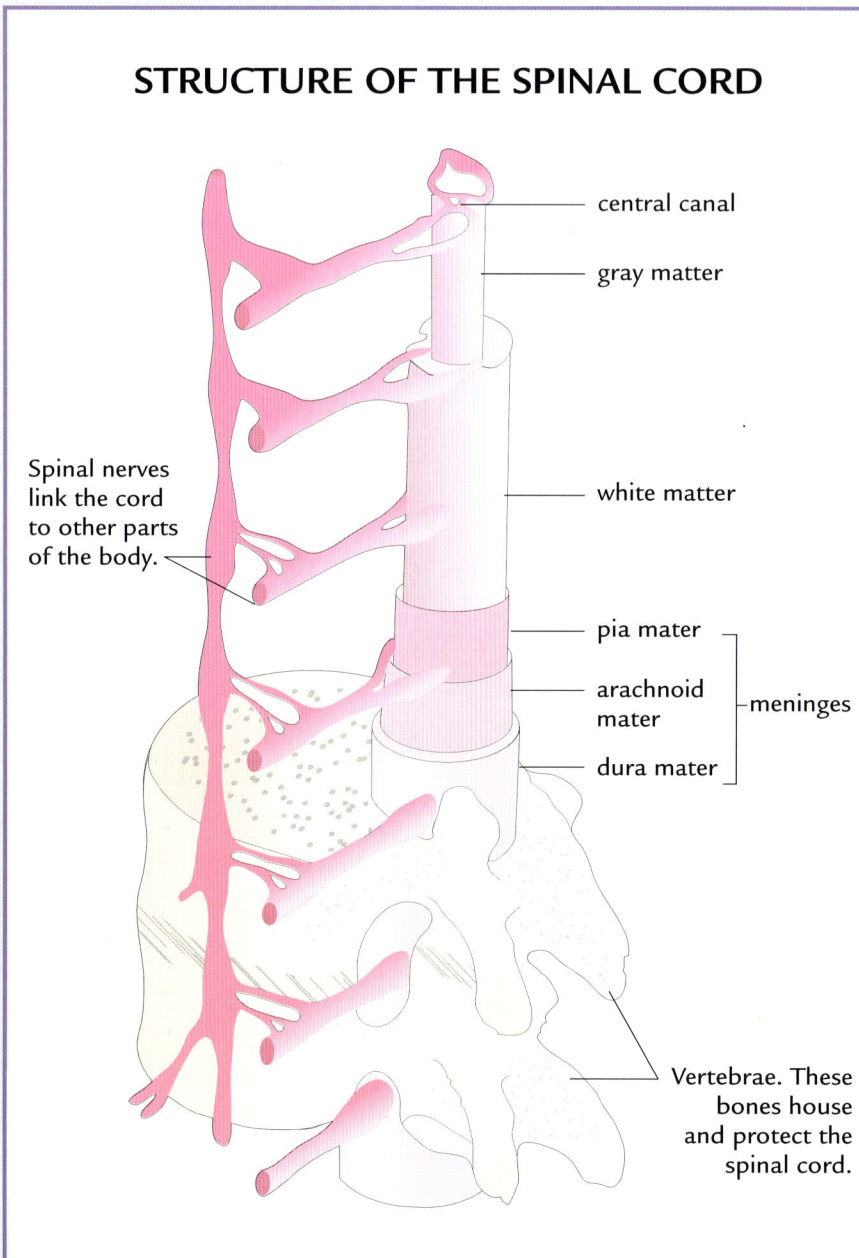

STRUCTURE OF THE SPINAL CORD

- central canal
- gray matter
- white matter
- pia mater
- arachnoid mater
- dura mater
- meninges
- Spinal nerves link the cord to other parts of the body.
- Vertebrae. These bones house and protect the spinal cord.

◀ A section through the spinal cord. White and gray matter make up the cord. These are surrounded by membranes called meninges.

system. The somatic system is concerned with the outside world and your reactions to it. It gathers information from your sense organs and sends this information to the CNS. It also carries signals from the CNS to the muscles attached to parts of your skeleton, allowing you to make conscious movements.

The autonomic system regulates the internal workings of your body. It carries information from the body to the CNS and transmits signals from the brain to organs such as the heart. Nerve cells that carry information toward the CNS are called sensory neurons. Those that carry signals from the CNS to organs such as muscles are called motor neurons.

The Nervous System

Reflexes

To a large extent your nervous system works automatically by reflex action. A reflex is a predictable, automatic response of the nervous system to an event (called a stimulus) outside or inside the body. Many reflexes operate by means of nerve connections in the spinal cord and do not require any conscious involvement of the brain.

Most reflexes are defense mechanisms that protect you against injury, such as withdrawing your hand when it touches a hot surface. Some reflexes, such as blinking your eye, work by means of nerve cell connections in parts of your brain.

The brain

Your brain is a soft, rounded mass about the size of a large grapefruit. It contains two main types of tissue, called gray matter and white matter. Gray matter is mainly made up of the cell bodies of billions

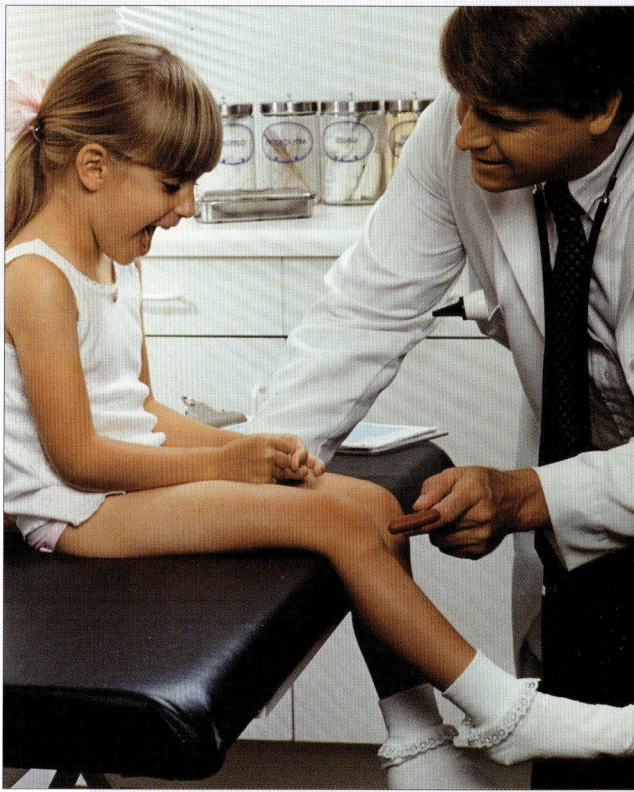

▲ This physician is testing the reflexes of a patient. A sharp tap just below the kneecap leads to a "knee-jerk" reflex.

TRY THIS

TESTING RESPONSE TIMES

Hold a ruler at one end, and let it hang down vertically. Have a friend put his or her hand near the bottom of the ruler with the thumb and forefinger ready to grasp it but not touching it. Tell your friend that you will drop the ruler sometime within the next 5 seconds and that he or she must try to catch it as fast as possible. Record the place at which he or she catches the ruler. This measurement will give you an idea of your friend's response time. Try this three or four times, and figure out an average response time for your friend. Then reverse roles, and test your own response time. Is the result much different between you and your friend? Try the same test at different times of day—in the morning and in the evening—to see if there is any difference in the results.

BIOLOGY MATTERS! The Human Body

HOW DO NERVES WORK?

RESTING STAGE

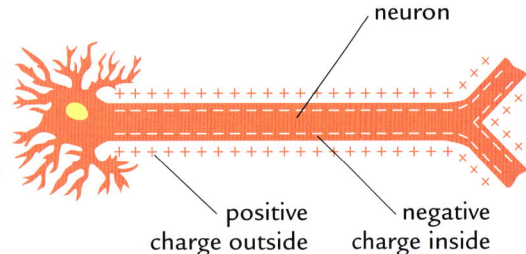

In its resting state the inside of a neuron is negatively charged. That is due to the presence of negative particles, or ions.

DEPOLARIZATION

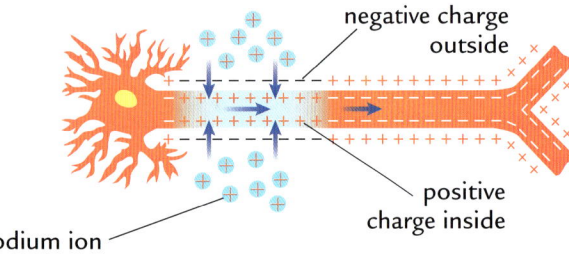

During a nerve impulse positive ions of sodium flood in. They switch the charge inside the cell to positive. This depolarization sweeps along the neuron.

REPOLARIZATION

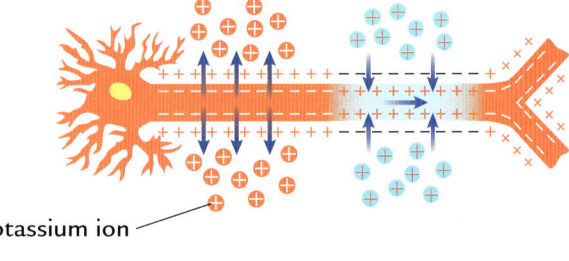

Once the impulse passes, positive potassium ions move out of the cell. This repolarization makes the inside of the cell negative again.

of interconnected nerve cells. White matter consists mainly of nerve cell fibers—cabling that connects different parts of the brain. Protective glial cells are distributed throughout the brain.

At the base of the brain is a structure called the brainstem. This stalklike organ connects the brain to the spinal cord. The brainstem is made up of three parts called the medulla, the pons, and the midbrain. The brainstem helps regulate automatic body functions such as the heartbeat and breathing. Behind the brainstem is a structure called the cerebellum. This structure helps control posture and balance, and it also coordinates movements. Thanks to your cerebellum, you can stand upright, keep your balance, and move around.

The uppermost and largest part of the brain is called the cerebrum. It is split into two halves called the cerebral

TRY THIS

FEEL YOUR FUNNY BONE

Your "funny bone" is actually a nerve called the ulnar nerve. To feel it, bend your left arm, and feel the tip of your elbow with your right hand. Running through the space between the elbow tip and a smaller bony lump below it, you will feel a firm cord—the ulnar nerve. Push the cord gently. You will feel a similar (though less painful) sensation as when you bump your "funny bone" against a hard object by accident.

The Nervous System

hemispheres. They are joined by a thick band of nerve cell fibers called the corpus callosum. The surface of each hemisphere is heavily folded, so the cerebrum looks a little like a huge walnut. The folds increase the area available for neurons. This outer part of the brain consists of gray matter and is called the cerebral cortex. The cortex is where advanced brain activities, such as thought and recognition of speech, take place.

Above the brainstem and between the two cerebral hemispheres are several other brain parts. They include the thalamus, which contains some areas involved in memory and movement; the pituitary gland, which produces many hormones (see 54–55)

HOT DEBATE

BRAIN CELL TRANSPLANTS

Surgeons have the capability of transferring human brain cells, a few million at a time, from one person's brain to another. That can help reduce the symptoms of certain brain illnesses. Scientists have also transplanted cells from the brains of pigs into humans.

There are many concerns regarding these transplants. Transported human brain cells are often tumor cells (cells growing out of control). However, scientists have developed a way of changing these rapidly dividing cells into nondividing ones before transplantation begins.

With pig cell transplants concerns have been raised that animals such as pigs may be turned into "spare parts" factories. There are also worries about new diseases being transferred from animals to humans.

▼ *This vertical slice through the brain shows the main structures inside.*

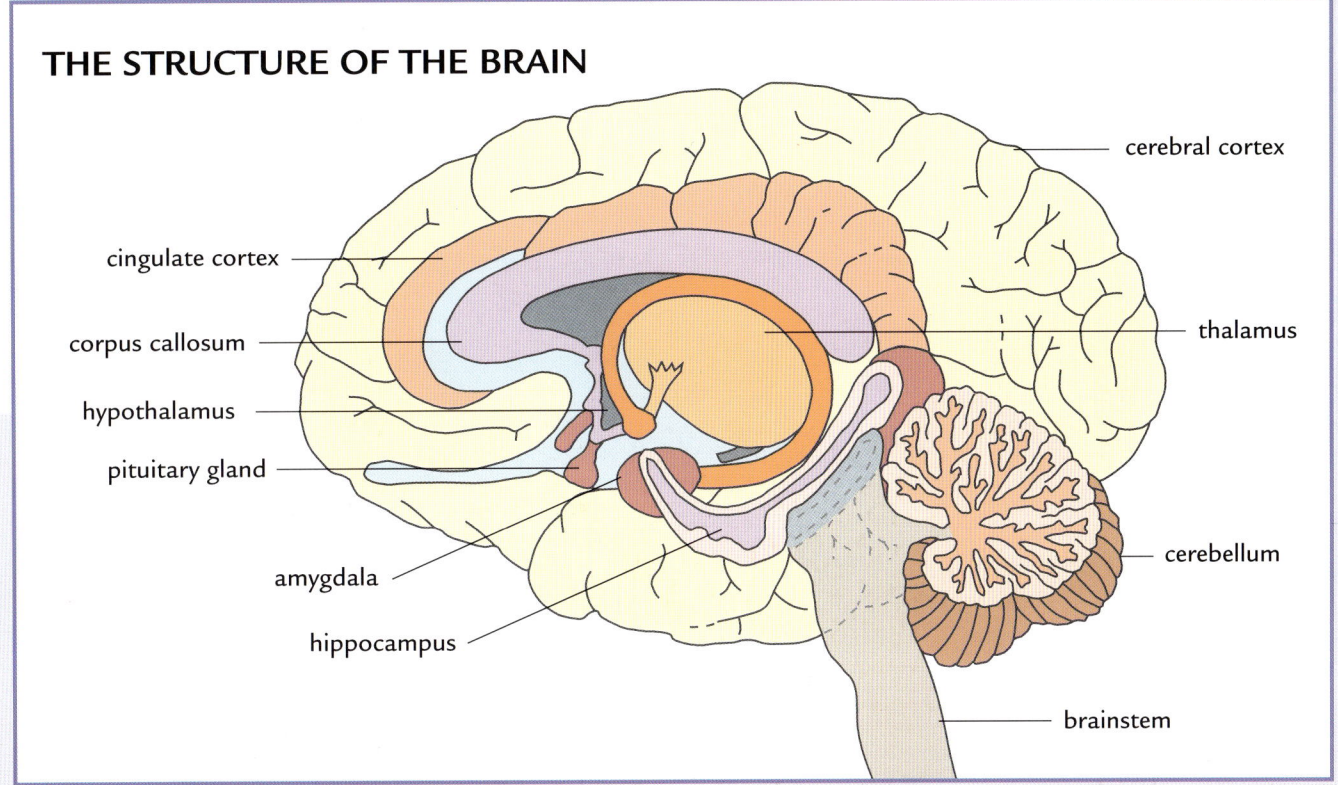

THE STRUCTURE OF THE BRAIN

- cingulate cortex
- corpus callosum
- hypothalamus
- pituitary gland
- amygdala
- hippocampus
- cerebral cortex
- thalamus
- cerebellum
- brainstem

BIOLOGY MATTERS! The Human Body

HOT DEBATE: BRAIN DEATH

The brainstem controls parts of the body such as the heart. With advances in medical technology physicians can sometimes keep these body parts working even when the brainstem has ceased to function. A new way of recognizing death, called brain death, was developed in the 1970s. Brain death occurs when the whole brain, including the brainstem, stops functioning, and there is no hope of getting it working again. Most doctors accept that a brain-dead person has died—there is no point in keeping that person's heart pumping. Others are uncomfortable with brain death since it goes against traditional ideas about death.

The brain uses up oxygen and nutrients at a fast rate in order to function, and for this reason it needs a large supply of blood. Numerous small blood vessels run throughout the brain. They are supplied by four large arteries that run up through the neck (see 18–25). If the blood supply to your brain were to be cut off for any reason, you would lose consciousness within ten seconds. After just a few minutes your brain would be permanently damaged.

and is an important part of the endocrine system; the hypothalamus, which forms a link between the nervous system and the endocrine system; and the limbic system, a collection of brain structures involved in functions such as memory, emotion, instinctive behavior, and sense of smell.

Lobes of the cortex

Each of the brain's hemispheres contains four main regions called lobes. They are the frontal

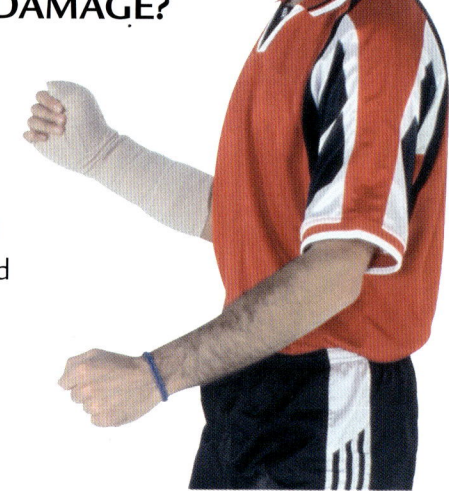

HOT DEBATE: DOES HEADING THE BALL CAUSE DAMAGE?

There have been some news reports of professional soccer players who have suffered brain damage that has lead to death as a result of "heading" the ball. Although this is a cause for concern, many of the affected people played soccer decades ago, when heavy leather balls were used. When wet, these balls grew heavier and heavier. The lighter soccer balls used today are much less risky. Experts say that to minimize any risk, soccer players should get instruction on how to head the ball correctly—with the forehead, not the top of the head—and children should use a size of ball appropriate to their age.

lobe (at the front), the occipital lobe (at the back), the temporal lobe (at the side), and the parietal lobe (on the upper side behind the frontal lobe). The cortex that covers each lobe has specific functions. For example, parts of the temporal lobe play a role in hearing; a large area of the frontal lobe (called the motor cortex) controls body movements; and a strip of the parietal lobe is involved in the sense of touch.

Different parts of the cortex often work together. For example, when you see someone you know, one part of the brain recognizes that person's face, and another finds the person's name in your memory. A third area analyzes your feelings about that person and whether you would like to call out a greeting. A fourth figures out the form of the greeting, and a fifth produces the exact sequence of nerve signals to muscles in your chest, neck, mouth, and lips to say "hello."

Some brain functions are shared equally between the two sides of the cerebrum. For example, there is a motor

▼ *Different functions of the brain take place at different locations on the cortex. This diagram also shows the four main lobes of the brain. The frontal lobe is yellow; the parietal lobe is pink; the temporal lobe is light blue; and the occipital lobe is dark blue.*

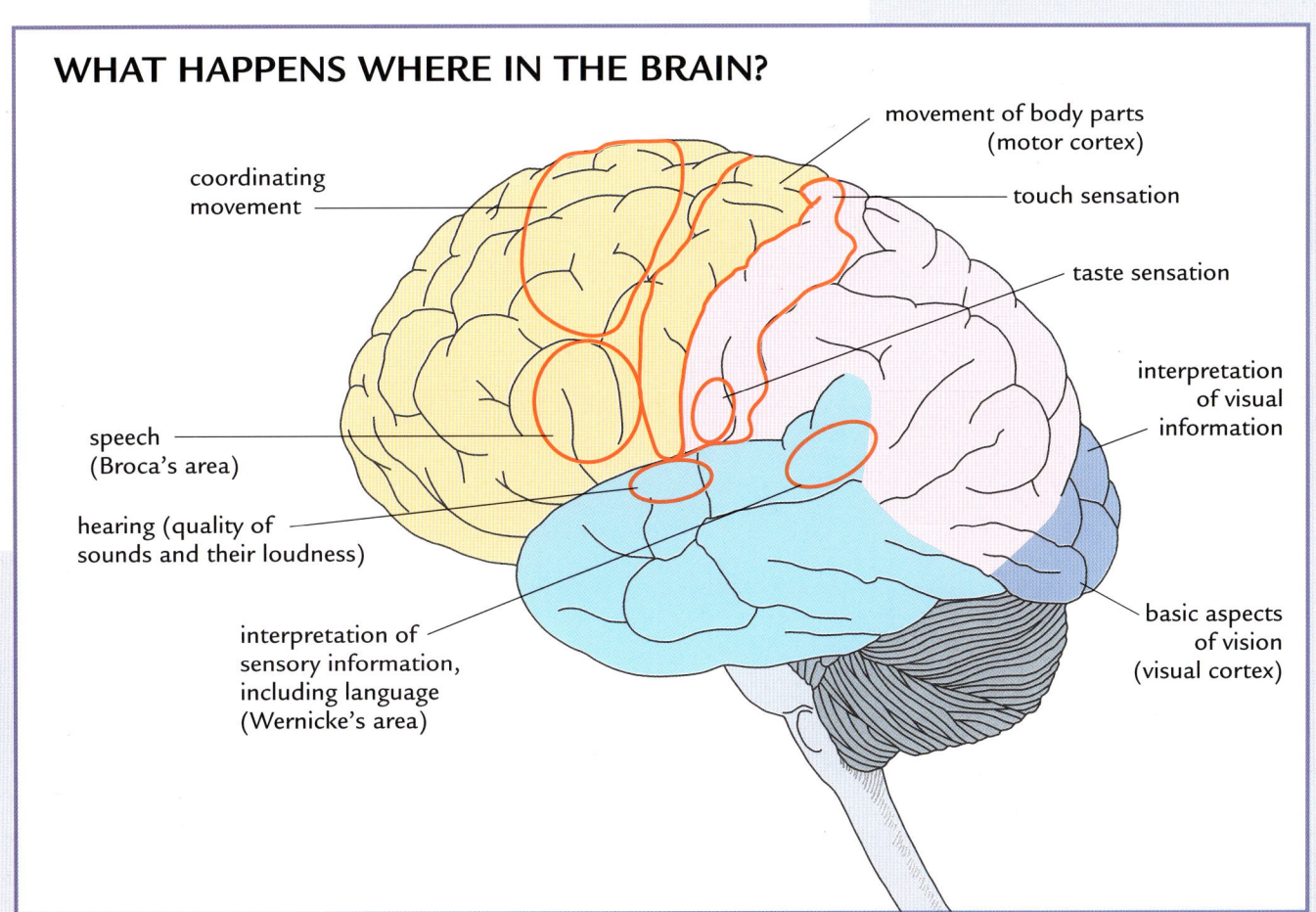

WHAT HAPPENS WHERE IN THE BRAIN?

BIOLOGY MATTERS! The Human Body

cortex on each side. Each motor cortex controls movements on the opposite side of the body. Other functions, such as language, are handled on one side of the brain called the dominant hemisphere. In nearly all right-handed people, and in about two-thirds of left-handed people, the left cerebral hemisphere is the dominant hemisphere. In most people the left hemisphere is also the one used for mathematical skills.

The nondominant hemisphere is important in spatial skills. People who suffer mild damage to the nondominant hemisphere may find they have problems when trying to read maps, or they may have trouble putting clothes on the right way around.

◀ *A complex activity, such as playing the piano, requires an enormous amount of nervous activity in the brain and in the rest of the nervous system.*

CLOSEUP
RIGHT OR LEFT

Most people are either right handed (86 percent) or left handed (9 percent), but 5 percent of people are ambidextrous—equally gifted with either hand. To test whether a young child is right or left handed, they are given a task, such as dealing a deck of cards or throwing a ball, to see which hand they use. As well as handedness, people also tend to be better with one foot, eye, and even ear than the other.

The Nervous System

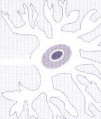

Memory and learning

One of the most important of your brain's functions is the ability to memorize information and later recall (bring back) this information from memory. Your brain retains a memory not just of facts, such as your name and home address, but also the meanings of those words and what those words sound and look like, the shapes and colors of objects, and so on. The brain also keeps a memory of events in your past and whether those events were pleasant or unpleasant, and it memorizes skills, such as how to walk or play the piano. The process of memorizing information and skills, and modifying those memories through experience, is called learning.

Scientists do not understand exactly how memories are stored in the brain, but they do know that there are two different types of memory storage systems.

TRICKING THE BRAIN

Cross your index and middle fingers on one hand to form a V shape. Now lightly rub the crossed tips of the two fingers up and down your nose. It will feel as if you have two noses! Your brain is confused by the information coming from the sides of the fingertips, which are in opposite positions from normal. To make sense of the information, the shape recognition area in your brain decides that two noses must be present!

Short-term memory is for information you have just been told, such as a phone number. It is limited and lasts only for a short time.

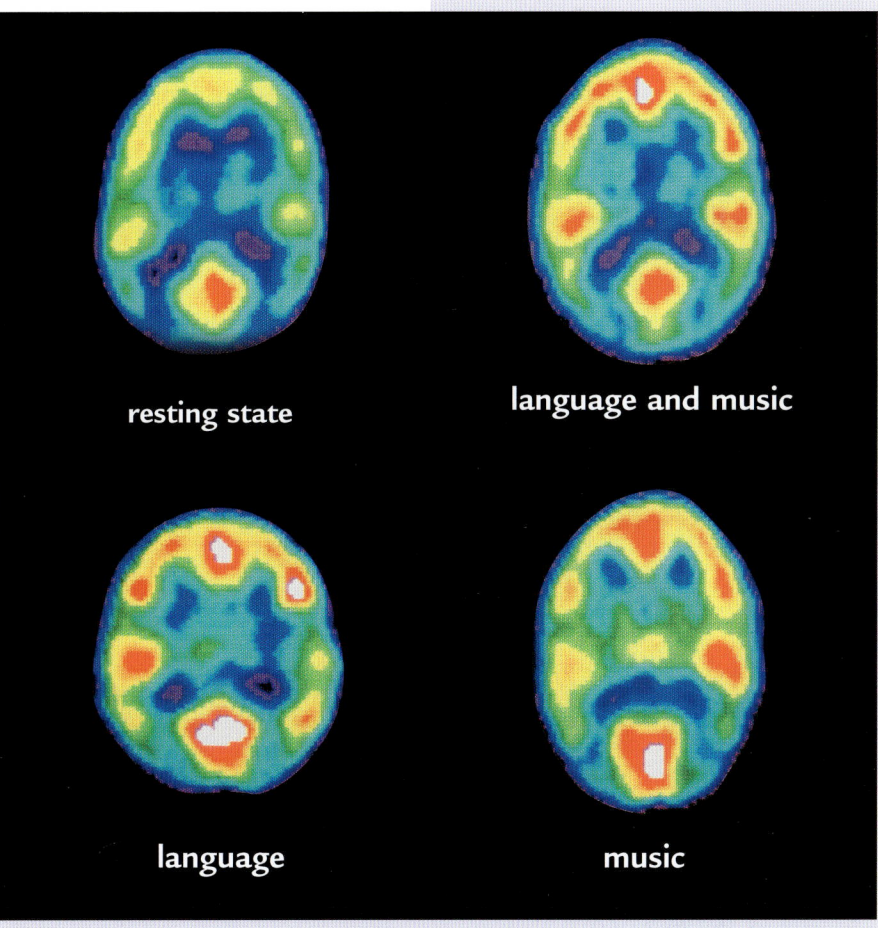

▶ These are scans showing brain activity. They show that different stimuli, such as music or spoken language, trigger activity in different parts of the brain.

TRY THIS

MEMORY AIDS

Your brain is better at storing information in visual form rather than, say, as strings of numbers. To remember something, it can help to fix an image in your mind related to the thing to be remembered. For example, to remember which months have 31 days, put your knuckles together. Then, starting on your first knuckle, count off the knuckles and spaces in between, saying the months in order. All the months with 31 days are on knuckles! Another trick can be to make up a phrase using the initial letters of words in the phrase to remember something. To remember the order of the classification groupings used in biology (kingdom, phylum, class, order, family, genus, species), you might use a phrase that conjures up an image, such as "*kings prefer chatting on fancy green sofas.*" This is called a mnemonic, or memory aid.

HOW THE PITUITARY GLAND WORKS

Nerve endings in the hypothalamus (see 48) release chemicals called neurohormones into capillary bed.

Blood flow carries neurohormones to anterior pituitary.

anterior (front) pituitary

capillary bed

posterior (back) pituitary

Neurohormones start or stop the release of hormones from the anterior pituitary.

Hormones are released and circulate around the body. These chemicals serve as messengers, controlling long-term processes. Many pituitary hormones trigger the release of other hormones elsewhere in the body.

Information about important events and skills or facts that you have learned by repetition go into a long-term memory bank. They generally stay with you for life.

The endocrine system

There is a close link between the nervous system and another information network, the endocrine system. The endocrine system consists of glands located in different parts of the body. They secrete chemicals called hormones into the bloodstream (see 18–25). Hormones act as "messenger" chemicals. As they spread through the body, they have specific effects on target tissues. These tissues are a long way away from the gland that released the hormone. Like

The Nervous System

APPLICATIONS

NERVOUS SYSTEMS AND ROBOTS

The study of nervous systems is playing an increasing part in the design of robots. Robots have become more complex, with ever more sophisticated sensory systems and interconnected moving parts. Designers are finding it ever more challenging to build electronic systems that can handle and integrate all the different inputs and outputs. So they are studying systems that already cope with such challenges—the nervous systems of living organisms. Scientists are particularly interested in unraveling mechanisms that enable animal movement to be so smooth and coordinated.

This is a spider-bot. Its walking is controlled by a system similar to the human nervous system. This robot has been designed to walk on the surface of other planets.

the nervous system, the endocrine system is a control system. However, the endocrine system mostly regulates longer-term processes than those controlled by the nervous system. Examples of processes under endocrine control include growth and reproduction (see **8**: 54–61), the storage and use of energy in the body (see **2**: 30–43), the rate of blood cell production, and the maintenance of the body's water balance.

Much of the functioning of the endocrine system is controlled by the hypothalamus and the pituitary gland in the brain. Blood vessels carry hormones from the hypothalamus to the front part of the pituitary gland, where they trigger the release of other hormones. They in turn may cause other glands in the body to release hormones of their own. The back part of the pituitary also releases a number of hormones.

7 Detecting the World

▲ A person who has lost the sense of sight is guided by a specially trained dog. Deaf people are also helped by dogs that have been taught to alert them to sounds such as the doorbell ringing.

One of your body's most important functions is to make you aware of things that are happening all around you. Detecting changes in the world is the job of the senses, which are controlled by the brain.

The human body has developed five different ways of detecting information about the world. We call them the five senses, and they are sight, hearing, smell, taste, and touch.

The first four of the senses are concentrated within single organs of the body. The fifth sense, touch, is unique since it

Detecting the World

is carried out by sensitive cells throughout the whole body, especially the skin.

Detecting, or sensing, the world involves more than just the body's sense organs and sensitive cells. The nervous system carries the information that the senses detect to the brain. The brain is the body's nerve center, and it is constantly interpreting a large amount of sensory information and figuring out how to respond. A very large part of detecting what is happening in the world occurs in the brain rather than in the sense organs themselves.

Seeing

The eyes are by far the most complex and important sense organs. You have two eyes. The brain combines the two slightly different images each

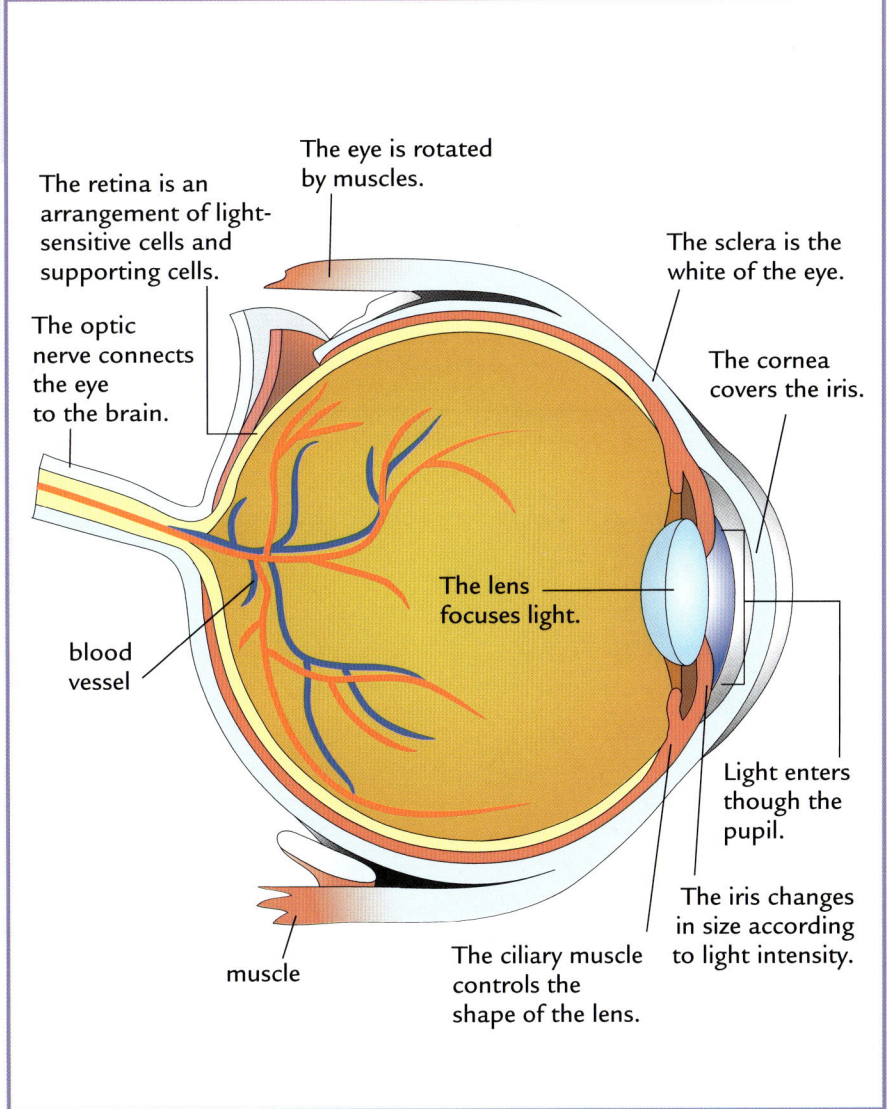

The retina is an arrangement of light-sensitive cells and supporting cells.

The eye is rotated by muscles.

The sclera is the white of the eye.

The optic nerve connects the eye to the brain.

The cornea covers the iris.

The lens focuses light.

blood vessel

Light enters though the pupil.

The iris changes in size according to light intensity.

muscle

The ciliary muscle controls the shape of the lens.

HOT DEBATE

HOW MANY SENSES?

Most people believe they have only five senses, but it is possible there may be as many as 15 senses or more. While the classic five senses are concerned with detecting the outside world, the other senses tell the brain what is happening inside the body. Feelings such as hunger, tiredness, and balance are examples of these internal sense mechanisms. Small organs in the inner ear control balance. They detect movements of your head and feed signals back to your brain so it can order muscles in your body to move and help you keep your balance.

BIOLOGY MATTERS! The Human Body

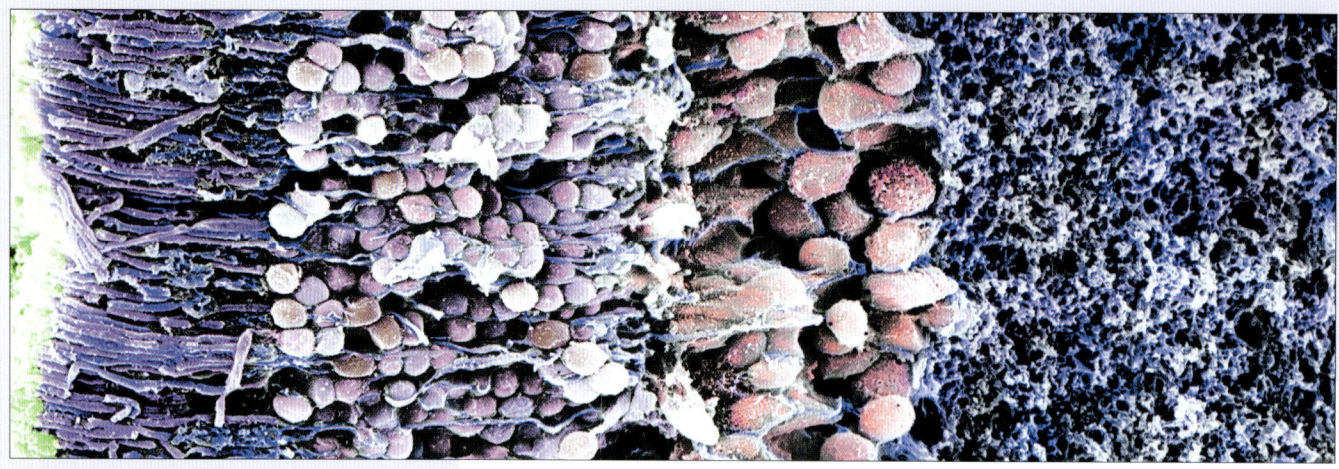

▲ The retina lines the eyeball and is a very complicated system of nerve cells. It is made up of three layers. The first layer of light-sensitive cells, which contains rods and cones, is connected by two main branches of cells to another layer of cells that lead to the optic nerve.

eye generates to make a single, three-dimensional (3-D) view of the world. This is called stereoscopic or binocular vision. Each eye is made up of an eyeball attached to six different muscles that rotate the eyeball in a socket within the skull.

The eyeball works in a similar way as a camera. Light goes through the cornea, a transparent outer lens of the eye, and the pupil, the black opening in the colored iris. The light is bent by a lens, travels through the vitreous humor (a clear gel that keeps the eyeball spherical), and arrives at the retina, a structure at the back of the eye.

The retina is like the photographic film in a camera. Sensory information from the retina is carried by the optic nerves (one from each eye) to the cerebral visual cortex, the part of the brain that decodes visual information (see 51). Together we call the eyes, the optic nerves, and the visual cortex the "visual system."

The retina is packed with two main types of cells. Some are shaped like rods and some like cones. These two cell types can detect different kinds of light. There are roughly 120 million rods and around six million cones. The

APPLICATIONS

MACHINES THAT CAN SEE

One reason for studying human vision is to help design computers and robots that can "see." Many automatic processes, from sorting mail to examining tissue samples for cancer, are now carried out with the help of electronic vision. Electronic vision systems have two main parts in much the same way as human vision. One is a digital camera that detects light and translates it into an electronic code, much as our eyes detect light and send electrical nerve impulses to the brain. The other part is a computer system that analyzes the code and figures out what they are—it is like the visual cortex of our brain (see 51).

Detecting the World

APPLICATIONS

NIGHT SIGHT

Police officers and soldiers use night vision cameras to help them see in the dark. Just as your eyes are sensitive to the light things give off, these cameras detect an invisible kind of light called infrared radiation. Animals or people are warmer than their surroundings and show up as red or purple on infrared cameras. The hand in the picture (right) is warmer than the object it is holding so it shows up as red and purple.

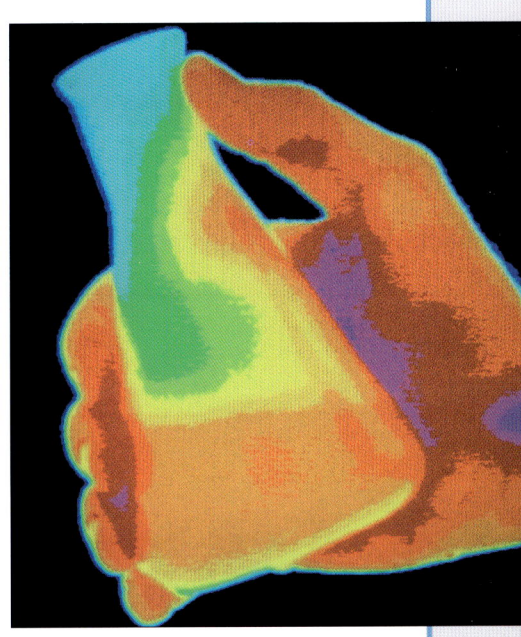

rods are sensitive mainly to gray shades and dim light, while the cones are sensitive to colored light. There are three types of cones, and each one is filled with a chemical that makes it most sensitive to either red, blue, or green light. The rods and cones are not distributed randomly over the retina. Most of the cones are packed into the center of the retina, called the fovea. The rods are arranged around the edge of the retina. That explains why your eyes see colors clearly in the center of what you look at (where there are most cones), and why you see dim objects or faint movements at the edges (where there are mostly rods).

▶ *With lights of the three primary colors of red, blue, and green you can get all the colors of a rainbow. Also, when lights of the three colors are mixed you see white light.*

TRY THIS

TEST YOUR RODS

Stare straight ahead. Without moving your head or eyes, concentrate on the things at the very edges of your field of view. You should not really be able to figure out the colors or shapes of these things, because that part of your vision is controlled by rod cells. Rods are poor at seeing details, and they do not detect colors.

BIOLOGY MATTERS! The Human Body

TRY THIS

REACHING OUT

Sit in front of a table that has different objects on it. Close one eye. Now without moving your head, try to reach out and touch different objects. Two eyes help us judge distances and locate things. See how much harder this is when you are using only one eye.

If the visual system is damaged in some way, the result can be anything from disrupted sight to complete blindness. Cataracts are a common eye problem in which part of the lens stops letting the light through due to old age, injuries, or poor diet. People who are color-blind have trouble telling some colors apart because they lack one or more of the three types of cone cells.

Damage to parts of the brain that process visual information can lead to conditions called agnosias. People with an agnosia can see objects because their eyes work, but do not recognize the objects because the visual cortex in their brain is damaged.

Hearing
Hearing is an essential part of human communication. Without hearing it is not possible to detect speech or listen to music. Just as your two eyes produce a three-dimensional landscape of the world, so your two ears generate a kind of three-dimensional "soundscape." In this soundscape you can easily locate sounds, such as someone calling out your name.

Like the visual system, the auditory (or hearing) system has sense organs (the two ears), connections between the brain and the sense organs (the auditory nerves), and a

HEARING SYSTEM

Pressure waves pass through the auditory canal and vibrate the tympanic membrane (eardrum).

The ossicles transmit vibrations of the tympanic membrane to the oval window of the cochlea.

The cochlea contains a liquid. When it receives vibrations, the nerve endings send signals to the brain to be interpreted.

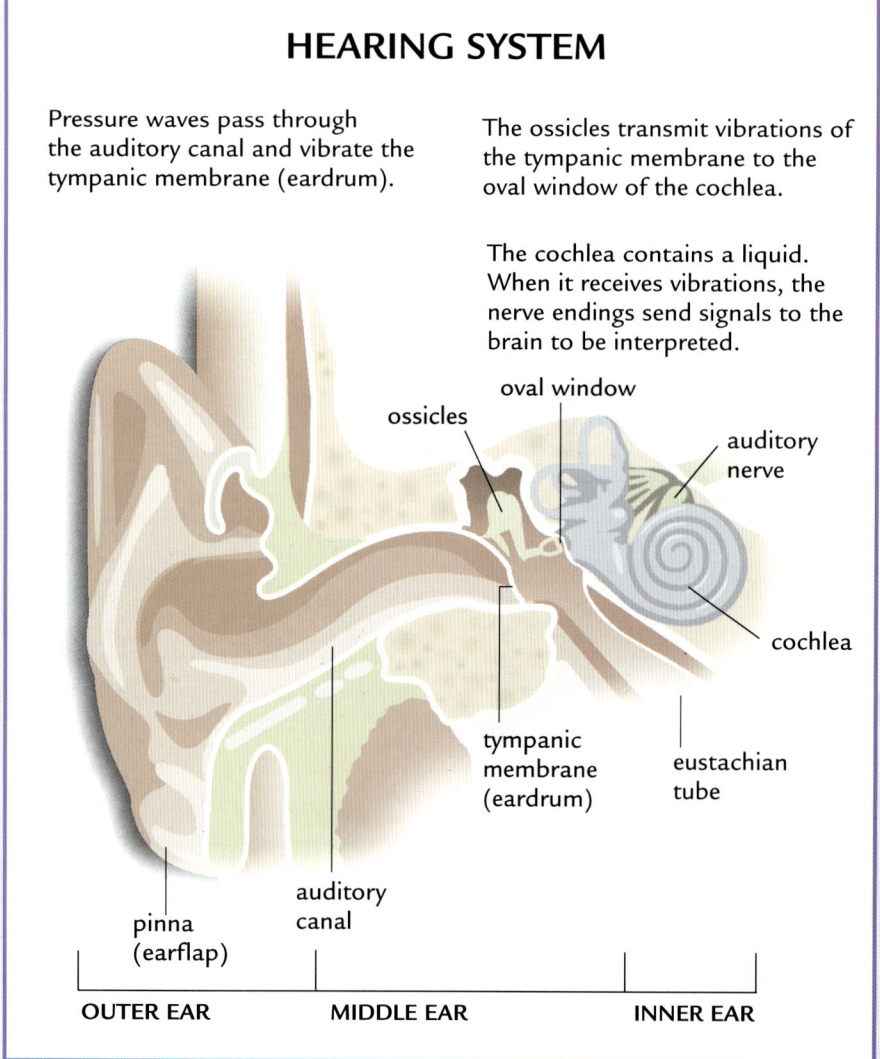

part of the brain with the job of processing sounds from the ears (the auditory cortex).

The ear itself has three main parts: the outer ear, the middle ear, and the inner ear. The fleshy, outer part is called the pinna or auricle. It collects sounds and channels them down a curved pipe, called the auditory canal, toward a structure called the tympanic membrane (eardrum).

When sound waves enter the ear, they make the air move back and forth in the auditory canal, and that causes the eardrum to vibrate. Three small bones called the malleus (hammer), incus (anvil), and stapes (stirrup), which look a bit like the objects they are named for, are connected to the eardrum, and they vibrate as well. Their vibrations are carried through a tiny membrane called the oval window to the passage and structures of the inner ear. The most important part of the inner ear is a structure shaped like a snail shell called the cochlea, which is filled with fluid and has 15,000 sensitive hairs on its walls. As sound vibrations travel from the oval window to the cochlea, they make the fluid move. The hairs detect the movement of the fluid and generate nerve impulses

TRY THIS

EAR TRUMPET

Go out in the street or a place where there are plenty of sounds to hear. Cup your hands behind your ears, and see how much more you can hear. Now make a funnel from rolled up paper, and leave a hole in the small end. Carefully put the small end to your ear. You should be able to hear even more now. Hearing aids in the 18th century (below) were similar to this. They were called ear trumpets.

BIOLOGY MATTERS! The Human Body

APPLICATIONS

HEARING AIDS

Modern hearing aids for deaf people are made up of tiny microphones and loudspeakers. They are positioned in the outer ear to increase the volume of sounds. Profoundly deaf people tend to have severe damage to the cochlea in their inner ear. Their hearing can be partially restored by embedding a type of hearing aid known as a cochlear implant inside their head (see below). Sounds are picked up by a microphone and carried to the speech processor. It translates the sounds into electrical signals that then go to the transmitter and on to the implanted stimulator. The stimulator sends the signals to the auditory nerve, and the brain interprets the sounds.

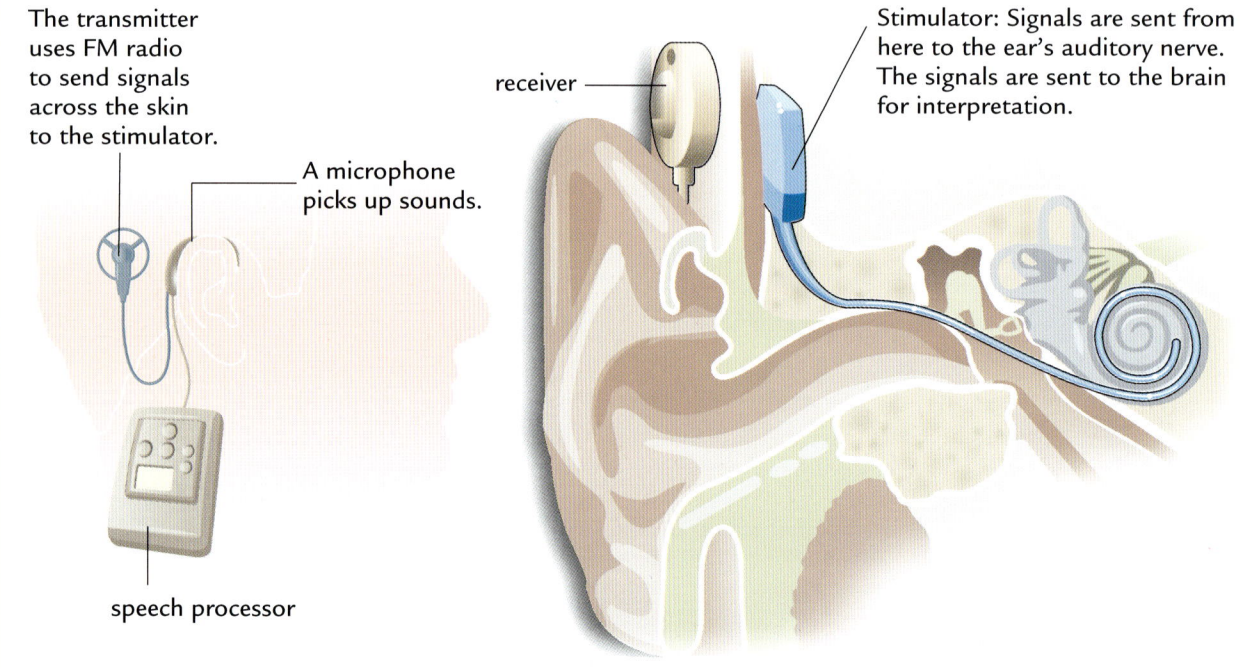

The transmitter uses FM radio to send signals across the skin to the stimulator.

A microphone picks up sounds.

speech processor

receiver

Stimulator: Signals are sent from here to the ear's auditory nerve. The signals are sent to the brain for interpretation.

in the auditory nerve. The nerve carries the signals to the brain, which interprets them as recognizable sounds.

The other senses

Touch, taste, and smell are other vital senses. Touch or feeling comes from sensitive nerve endings in the skin and from the hairs nearby. They respond to factors of pressure, pain, and temperature. Taste comes from taste buds, which are extremely sensitive bumps on the tongue (see opposite). Smell is detected by seven types of receptor cells inside

Detecting the World

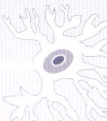

 **TRY THIS**

THE SMELL OF TASTE

Next time you eat a meal, try this experiment. Close off your nostrils just by holding your nose. Make sure you cannot smell. Now try tasting different types of foods. You may find they do not taste the same as usual. Smell plays a major part in how we taste things. If your nose is blocked when you have a cold, food seems tasteless.

the nose that are sensitive to roughly seven different types of smells. The receptor cells send signals down the olfactory (smell) nerves to parts of the brain that specialize in recognizing smells (see right).

THE TONGUE

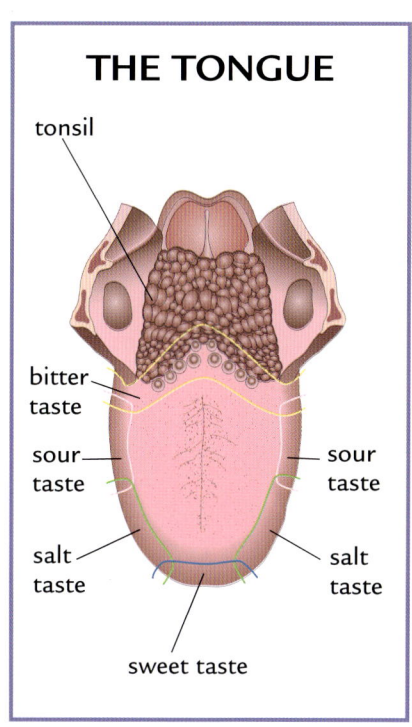

▲ *Different areas of the tongue are most sensitive to one of four basic tastes: sweet, salt, sour, and bitter.*

THE NASAL CAVITY

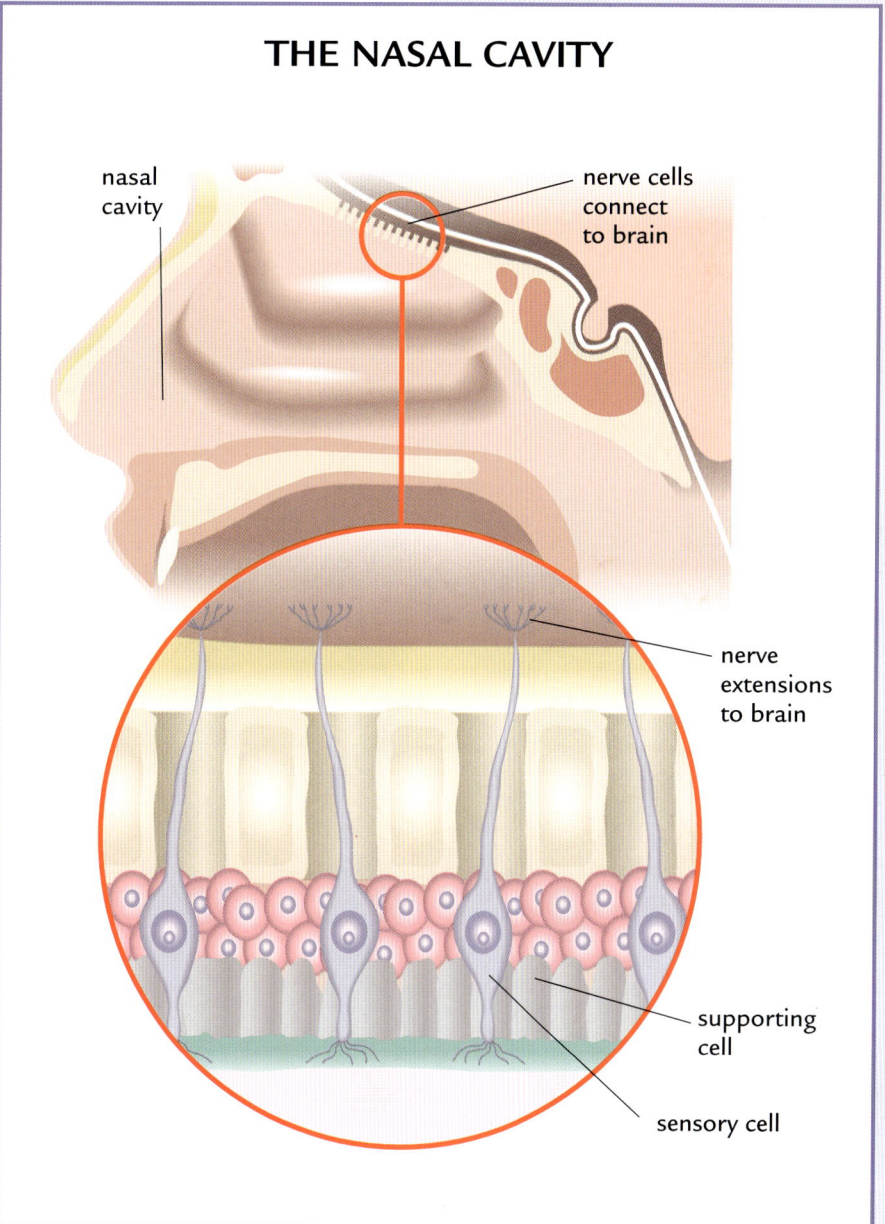

8 Health and Defense

Usually it is only when something goes wrong with our body that we appreciate how important good health is.

Thankfully we have a complex group of cells and organs called the immune system that protects us from many diseases. We can also reduce the risk of illness by leading a healthy lifestyle.

Over the last 100 years or so the length of time people can generally expect to live (also called the life expectancy) and the effects of diseases have altered dramatically as lifestyles and environments have changed. At the start of the 20th century many people

◀ A health worker gives a vaccine containing inactive disease organisms to a child. More than 80 percent of U.S. children are vaccinated against certain diseases.

Health and Defense

died before the age of 50. Many children died through infectious diseases such as measles. Today the average life expectancy in the United States is more than 75 years, and childhood deaths are relatively rare.

Improvements in diet, medicine, and hygiene during the 20th century played a crucial role in increasing life expectancy. Antibiotic medicines, which kill bacteria, and immunization programs (see 66) reduced the number of deaths due to infectious disease. Today medicines that prepare the body for future infections called vaccines protect 80 percent of all children.

By contrast with a century ago, the major causes of death today in wealthy countries are cancer, heart disease, strokes, diabetes, and smoking-related diseases. Most of these illnesses stem from the way people live their lives. It is possible to reduce the risk of contracting many of the diseases that are caused by bad habits by altering diet, exercising more, and not smoking. Another major

TRY THIS

WHAT DO YOU EAT?

The typical U.S. diet contains too much fat, salt, and sugar. This kind of diet has been linked to the most common causes of death in the United States—cancer and heart disease. People are often unaware that they eat too much of certain food types, since food producers add extra ingredients to make them taste better. List all the foods you eat in one day. Check the package labels for sugar, fats (they may be called lipids), and salt (it may be called sodium). Most packages indicate the amount of each per 100g of the total contents. Find out whether you are eating more of each than you should.

Black tar deposits in a lung, caused by smoking cigarettes.

WHAT DO YOU THINK?

SMOKING AND RELATED DISEASES

In many countries smoking is the main cause of death in people under the age of 65. Smoking causes lung cancer, and it can also increase the risk of developing other cancers, heart disease, and strokes. Tobacco smoke contains many substances, such as tar and carbon monoxide, that are poisonous to the body. Tar coats and irritates the linings of the lungs. Carbon monoxide attaches to red blood cells in place of oxygen. There are many other chemicals in cigarettes that cause cancer, too.

Why do you think people start smoking in the first place? Why do you think they continue to smoke, often for many years, despite the risks to their health?

BIOLOGY MATTERS! The Human Body

THE INFLAMMATORY RESPONSE

▶ A splinter bursts through the skin, bringing bacteria into the body. Damaged cells under the skin release a chemical called histamine. It moves into the bloodstream and alerts the immune system.

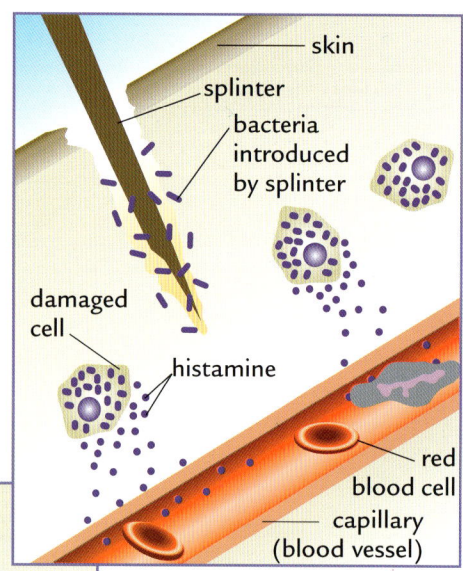

◀ The histamine causes the capillary to become leaky and to expand a little. Complement proteins move from the blood toward the cells. These proteins attract white blood cells called phagocytes.

▶ The phagocytes engulf and destroy the bacteria and the damaged cells. Then histamine release stops, and complement protein levels fall. Phagocytes are no longer attracted, and the tissue returns to normal.

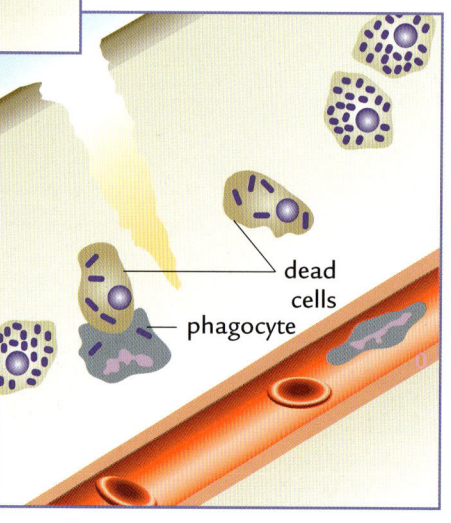

cause of death and disability today is traffic and other kinds of accidents.

Lines of defense

Agents of disease such as bacteria and viruses that enter the body are called pathogens. People come into contact with pathogens, as well as chemical toxins, all the time. However, thanks to the work of body's immune system, only very few of these harmful things succeed in making us ill.

There are three main lines of defense in the immune system. The first is the body's barriers—the skin and the membranes that cover entry points for pathogens, such as the eyes, nose, and mouth.

The second line of defense lies inside the body (see left). It involves mostly white blood cells called phagocytic cells, proteins called antibodies that attack pathogens (see 1: 33), and a process known as the

Health and Defense

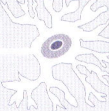

HOW DOES IMMUNIZATION WORK?

Most children in America are immunized against a number of diseases, such as diptheria, pertussis, and polio. During immunization a vaccine that contains a small amount of weakened or inactive disease organisms is introduced into your body. This is usually done by injection, although some vaccines are swallowed. The vaccine stimulates your immune system to produce antibodies (see 69). They are able to recognize and act against the disease organism.

Should you come into contact with the active form of the disease later in life, the antibodies will provide protection.

inflammatory response. The first and second lines of defense are general ways of protecting the body against different kinds of pathogens. However, there is a third and final line of defense that is able to recognize, destroy, and remember specific pathogens even if they enter the body again years later.

Through the barricades

The role the skin plays in the immune system is similar to that of an ancient city wall—it is a barrier against potential invaders. Unless the skin is pierced or damaged in some way, viruses or bacteria cannot normally penetrate it. Human skin also uses chemical weaponry to halt intruders. It produces acidic substances that make the skin hostile to many microorganisms.

Membranes line various parts of the body that are open to the air. Membranes inside the nose, for example, contain cells that produce a slimy substance called mucus. It traps microorganisms, and tiny hairlike filaments called cilia sweep the mucus and the microorganisms down into the throat to be swallowed. They then pass into the gut, where they are broken down.

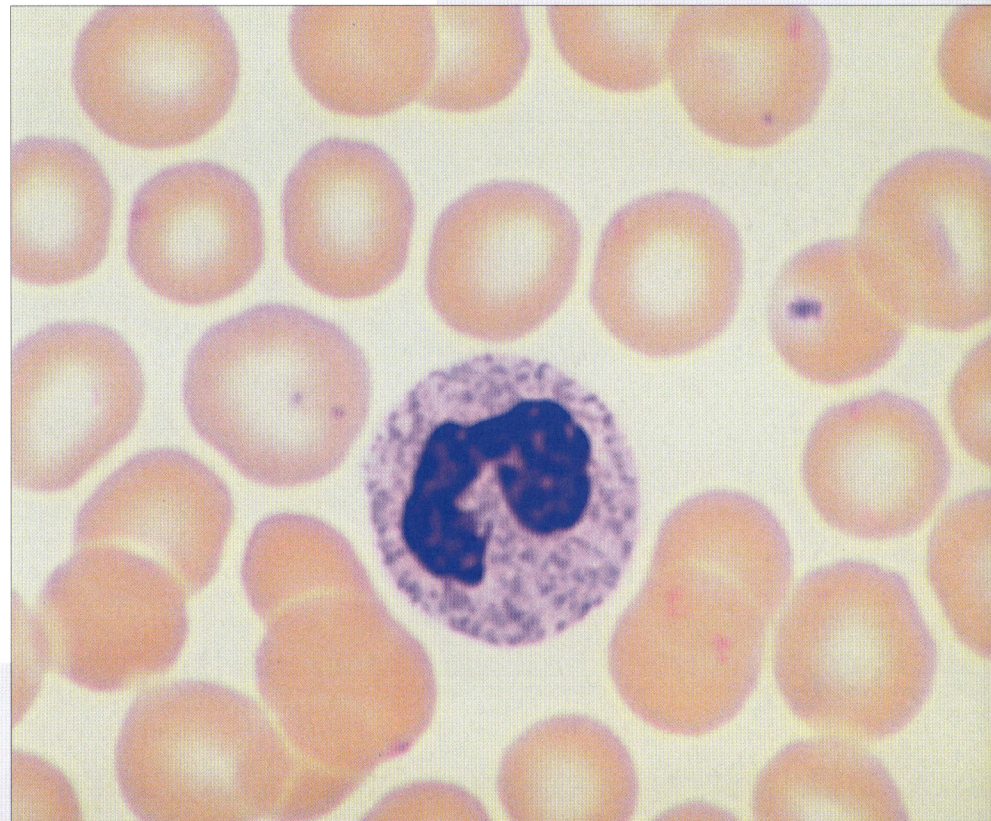

▼ A neutrophil surrounded by red blood cells. These important white blood cells are very mobile, moving swiftly through the blood to destroy pathogens.

BIOLOGY MATTERS! The Human Body

HOT DEBATE

THE MMR JAB

Rather than using three injections, measles, mumps, and rubella are often immunized against all at once. This so-called MMR jab has been largely accepted in the United States, but its use remains controversial in Europe. Health authorities insist that the jab is safe.

Many members of the public, however, are convinced that the MMR jab can lead to psychological disorders such as autism. They accuse the health authorities of putting profit (since the single jab is cheaper than a course of three) before safety.

Should a pathogen enter the body, through a cut, for example, it must deal with the second line of defense inside the body. The area around the infection becomes red and inflamed. This is the inflammatory response, in which the blood supply to the area increases. That enables white blood cells, which are attracted by chemical signals released from body tissues under attack, to reach the area as quickly as possible.

Antipathogen crusaders

White blood cells called phagocytes are a key part of the second line of defense. They gobble up microorganisms and destroy them using strong chemicals. Phagocytes are produced in the bone marrow (see 37). There are several types of phagocytes. Neutrophils are the most common. They move to sites of infection, where they multiply and destroy bacteria and viruses. Their work done, the neutrophils die a few days later.

Neutrophils fight invaders with the help of a larger, longer-living, and much more powerful type of phagocyte called a macrophage. They

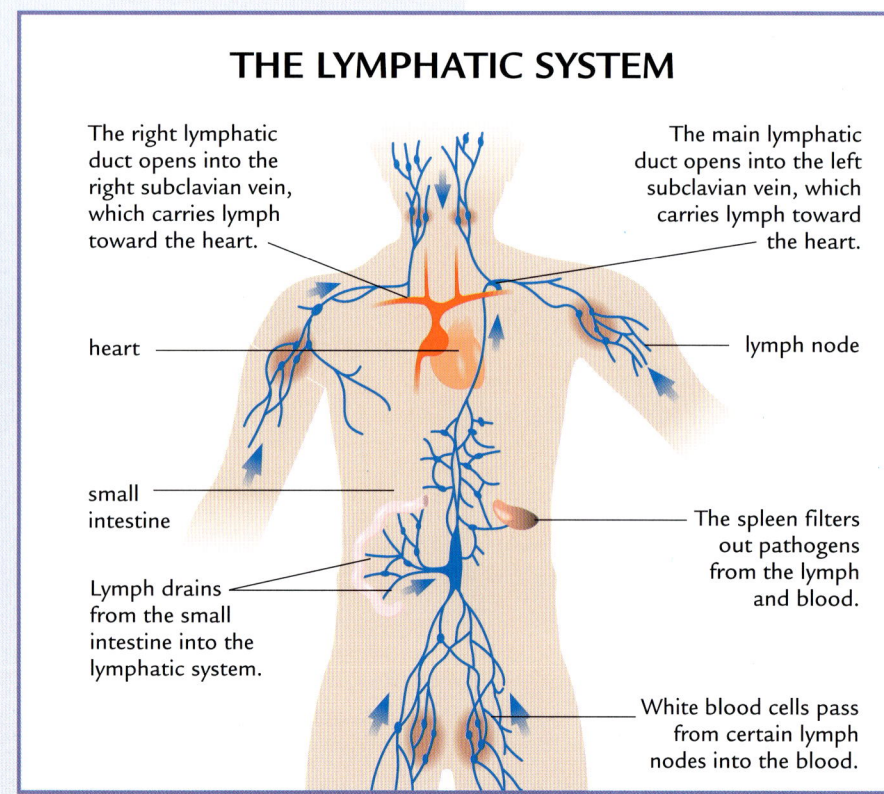

THE LYMPHATIC SYSTEM

The right lymphatic duct opens into the right subclavian vein, which carries lymph toward the heart.

heart

small intestine

Lymph drains from the small intestine into the lymphatic system.

The main lymphatic duct opens into the left subclavian vein, which carries lymph toward the heart.

lymph node

The spleen filters out pathogens from the lymph and blood.

White blood cells pass from certain lymph nodes into the blood.

◀ The human lymphatic system is shown in blue; other important organs and vessels are shown in red.

Health and Defense

are permanently present in many organs, where they constantly search for and destroy pathogens. Some float freely in the bloodstream and in lymph (fluid that bathes the body's cells), looking for intruders. Macrophages also clean up dead neutrophils.

Another type of phagocyte, called an eosinophil, targets larger parasites such as disease-causing worms. Body cells that grow abnormally or are infected by viruses are killed by another important cell, the natural killer cell.

Intelligent cells

The third and final line of defense centers around a type of white blood cell called a lymphocyte. Lymphocytes deal with most bacteria and viruses that enter the body. Like all white blood cells, lymphocytes develop in the bone marrow. However, unlike the others, lymphocytes are able to recognize and kill specific pathogens and then remember them in the future, allowing a swift and deadly response.

Some lymphocytes turn into cells called B cells, which are released straight into the bloodstream. During childhood other lymphocytes move through the bloodstream to the thymus, an organ in the chest. There they turn into cells called T cells.

B cells and T cells mostly occur in the lymphatic system. As in the circulatory system (see 18–25), the lymphatic system has vessels through which a liquid (lymph) flows. However, lymph is not pumped around

▼ *A specific antibody attacks just one type of pathogen.*

FIND YOUR LYMPH NODES

When you are ill, your lymph nodes become swollen because they are full of lymphocytes fighting pathogens. Lymph nodes occur throughout your body. They are heavily distributed in your neck and around your groin and armpits, for example. The next time you have a sore throat, feel the sides of your throat. They should feel bigger than usual and may be sore. Compare this to how they feel one week after the infection. By then they should have dropped in size.

THE SPECIFIC NATURE OF ANTIBODIES

1. These are *a* antibodies.

2. The *a* antibodies attack A foreign particles and make them harmless.

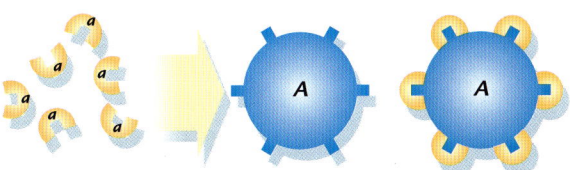

3. These are *b* antibodies.

4. The *b* antibodies attack B foreign particles and make them harmless.

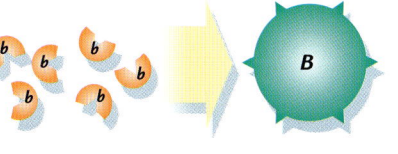

5. However, the *a* antibodies do not bind to proteins on foreign particle *B*, so they cannot attack it.

6. Similarly, the *b* antibodies do not bind to proteins on foreign particle *A*, so they cannot block it.

BIOLOGY MATTERS! The Human Body

APPLICATIONS: MAKING ANTIBODIES

Scientists have discovered how to boost immune systems by artificial means. In 1984 molecular biologists Cesar Milstein (born 1927) and Georges Köhler (1946–1995) won a Nobel Prize for inventing a technique to mass produce

A vet administers monoclonal antibodies to a newborn calf.

artificial antibodies. In 1998 these artificial (or monoclonal) antibodies were first used to treat breast cancer. Monoclonal antibodies are also used in pregnancy tests. They bind to a chemical that occurs inside pregnant women.

CLOSEUP: THE IMMUNE SYSTEM AND HIV

Some pathogens can trick the immune system. One of them is the HIV virus. This virus constantly alters the makeup of its outer surface, so phagocytes are unable to recognize it as a foreign body. The virus attacks white blood cells called helper T cells. It forces the helper T cell to make copies of its genes (see **3**: 26–37). That weakens the cell, which soon dies. With fewer and fewer helper T cells available, the immune system collapses. This disease is called AIDS.

---

the body by the heart as blood is. Lymph passes through the walls of capillaries, flows between the cells of organs, and is collected by a series of tiny lymph vessels. They carry the lymph back to the circulatory system along with the cells' waste products. The lymphatic system contains glands called nodes, where lymphocytes gather.

When they are needed, B cells turn into plasma cells. They in turn produce proteins called antibodies. Antibodies allow each specific B cell to detect and destroy a particular pathogen. Antibodies are Y-shaped proteins. Like a key fitting a lock, antibodies recognize and bind to proteins specific to the membranes of different pathogens. Plasma cells produce millions of antibodies at a time.

Unlike B cells, killer T cells attack body cells infected by a pathogen. Killer T cells recognize infected cells because they display proteins from the pathogen on their outer membranes once they have been infected. When it recognizes an infected cell, a killer T cell copies itself many times before attacking and destroying both cell and pathogen.

More Information

Books

Gilpin, D. *History of Invention: Medicine*. New York: Facts on File, Inc., 2004.

Kim, M. and Gold, S. D. *The Endocrine and Reproductive Systems*. Berkeley Heights, NJ: Enslow Publishers, 2003.

Llewellyn, C. *The Big Book of Bones*. New York: Peter Bedrick Books, 1998.

Royston, A. *Why Do I Get a Toothache?: And Other Questions about Nerves*. Chicago, IL: Heinemann Library, 2003.

Stangl, J. *What Makes You Cough, Sneeze, Burp, Hiccup, Blink, Yawn, Sweat, and Shiver?* New York: Franklin Watts, Inc., 2000.

VanCleave, J. *The Human Body for Every Kid: Easy Activities That Make Learning Science Fun*. New York: John Wiley & Sons, 1995.

Viegas, J. *The Heart: Learning How Our Blood Circulates*. New York: Rosen Publishing Group, 2002.

Walker, R. *Body Science: How We Breathe*. North Mankato, MN: Smart Apple Media, 2004.

Websites

Biology in Motion
biologyinmotion.com
Interactive online activities and 3-D animations on body topics such as fat digestion, the thyroid gland, and the cardiovascular system.

BodyQuest
library.thinkquest.org/10348
Take a tour of the human body, with many graphics, experiments, and a quiz for each body system.

Brain Connection
www.brainconnection.com
A site with articles, brain-building activities, animations, library, gallery, and an anatomy section.

The Heart Online
sln.fi.edu/biosci/index.html
Explore the heart, its development and structure. Follow blood through blood vessels, and learn how to have a healthy heart.

Kidshealth
www.kidshealth.org/kid/body/index.html
Illustrations, music, and lessons about your body at the "My Body" section. Learn how to stay healthy.

Sighting the First Sense
library.thinkquest.org/C001464/cgi-bin/view.cgi
Interactive demonstrations and unique resource about the eye and sight.

The Virtual Body
www.medtropolis.com/VBody.asp
Interactive, animated tour of the human body with "build-your-own" features.

Way Cool Surgery
www.waycoolsurgery.com
Videos of heart surgery, case histories, and information about medical careers and heart-disease prevention.

Glossary

alveolus Tiny air sac that forms bunches in the lungs through which exchange of oxygen and carbon dioxide takes place.

antibody Protein produced by white blood cells in response to an antigen; important in an immune response.

antigen Molecule (often on the surface of a foreign body) that the immune system can recognize.

aorta Major artery leading directly from the heart.

appendicular skeleton Part of the skeleton attached to the axial skeleton, including legs, pelvis, arms, and shoulders.

artery Branching vessels with elastic walls that carry blood from the heart around the body.

atrioventricular (AV) node Part of the heart that sends signals to slow down the SA node, allowing the contraction of the heart chambers to be regulated.

atrium One of a pair of heart chambers that receives blood before pumping it into a ventricle.

autonomic nervous system Part of the PNS that regulates the internal functions of the body automatically.

axial skeleton Part of the skeleton consisting of the skull, backbone, and rib cage.

bile A yellow fluid secreted by the liver; in the intestine it helps in the emulsification and absorption of fats.

Broca's area Part of the brain important for speech organization.

capillary Tiny, thin-walled blood vessels through which oxygen and nutrients pass into cells, with waste going the other way.

carbohydrates Sugar molecules important in respiration.

central nervous system (CNS) The brain and spinal cord and their supporting cells.

cochlea Coiled, fluid-filled structure in the inner ear that translates vibrations received at the tympanum into signals that go to the brain.

diffusion The movement of molecules of liquids and gases from points of high concentration to points of lower concentration.

digestion The breakdown by enzymes of food into small, easily absorbed molecules in the stomach.

emulsification The suspension of oil or fat droplets in water.

endocrine system System of glands that release hormones.

enzyme Protein that speeds up chemical reactions inside an organism.

exoskeleton Tough outer skin of animals such as insects, spiders, and crabs.

hemoglobin Pigment that occurs in red blood cells; binds to oxygen and carbon dioxide to carry these gases around the body.

hormone Chemical messenger that regulates life processes inside the body.

hypothalamus Part of the brain that releases chemicals that control the pituitary gland.

microvillus One of millions of hairlike structures that line the cells of the gut; they increase the surface area available for absorption.

mineral An inorganic (non-carbon-containing) substance essential in tiny amounts for nutrition.

Glossary

nephron An excretory unit of the kidney.

neuron A nerve cell.

osteoporosis A condition leading to brittle and fragile bones that mainly affects older women.

pepsin Enzyme in the stomach that breaks down proteins into polypeptides.

peripheral nervous system (PNS) A network of nerves that spreads from the central nervous system to the rest of the body.

peristalsis Waves of muscular contraction that ripple along the walls of the digestive system to keep food moving.

pituitary gland Gland in the brain that releases hormones. They control the output of other endocrine glands.

platelet Tiny disk in the blood that helps clotting.

pleura One of a pair of delicate saclike membranes that wrap around the lungs.

porpoising When animals such as dolphins and penguins leap from the water during fast swimming.

prosthesis An artificial device that replaces a missing body part, such as a limb.

red blood cell Cell that carries oxygen and carbon dioxide around the body.

respiration The liberation of energy from food using oxygen; occurs inside the cell.

retina Sensitive layer of cells at the back of the eye that is stimulated by light. It sends this visual information to the brain through the optic nerve.

rickets Disease caused by a lack of vitamin D.

saliva Liquid released by glands in the mouth. It helps lubricate food and also contains enzymes that begin the process of digestion.

sinoatrial (SA) node Part of the right atrium in the heart. Sends electrical impulses that regulate the heartbeat.

somatic nervous system Part of the PNS that gathers information from sensory organs and sends it to the central nervous system; also takes signals from the CNS to the muscles.

sphincter Ring of muscle that opens and closes entries to structures; found at the base of the stomach, for example.

tracheal system System of tubes used for breathing by most arthropods, such as insects.

tympanum Structure that receives sound vibrations in the air. Movements of the tympanum go to the cochlea after amplification by three inner ear bones and from the cochlea via nervous impulses to the brain.

vein Blood vessel that carries blood toward the heart from the capillaries.

vena cava Large vein that brings blood from the body into the heart.

ventricle One of a pair of heart chambers that receive blood from the atria. Blood from one is pumped to the lungs; blood from the other leaves via the aorta to move through the body.

vitamin An organic (carbon-containing) substance essential in tiny amounts for nutrition.

Wernicke's area Part of the brain important for interpreting language.

white blood cell Colorless blood cell that forms part of the immune system.

Set Index

Numbers in **bold** refer to volumes; page numbers in *italics* refer to picture captions.

A

adaptations **1**:12–13; **9**:23–25, 51
adaptive radiation **9**:49–50
ADHD **8**:61
aging **8**:62–70
alcohol **5**:51
algae **2**:9; **4**:6, 21, 22, 24, 28, 29; **5**:5; **8**:10
alleles **3**:6, 10, 11, 12–15, 42, 53, 54–55, 62; **8**:17; **9**:27, 33–34, 37, 38
allergies **3**:62
alternation of generations **5**:41–43, 69; **8**:36
amebas **2**:26–27; **3**:38; **4**:20, 22, 23, 25, 29
amino acids **1**:32–33; **7**:9
amniocentesis **3**:57
amphibians **6**:8, 23; **9**:58
anabolic reactions **1**:34, 35
antibiotics **2**:23; **4**:16, 54–55, 68–69; **9**:13
antibodies **1**:33–34; **4**:49; **7**:69, 70
ants **3**:44; **5**:22; **6**:46, 67
aphids **6**:46, 48, 68–69; **8**:15
appendix **1**:26–27
arteries **7**:23, 24
arthritis **8**:68
arthropods **1**:18
atmosphere **10**:22–23
atoms **1**:10, 11, 28
Australopithecus **6**:47; **9**:62, 63, 64–65
autopsies **1**:56
autotomy **6**:44, 45
auxin **5**:25, 26, 27, 29

B

bacteria **1**:7, 16; **4**:4, 8–19
  antibiotic-resistant **4**:16, 55, 60, 68–69; **9**:13
  artificial **1**:13
  cell walls **2**:23
  conjugation **8**:17
  and disease **4**:19, 44, 46, 48
  extreme lives **4**:6–7, 8, 11, 12
  flagella **2**:28
  in food production **4**:10, 11, 57–59
  and genetic engineering **3**:63–64, 65–66; **4**:60–63, 68
  genomes **3**:45–47
  grown on gel **1**:54
  light-producing **6**:59
  mining using **4**:69
  and plastics **1**:37; **4**:65
  and pollutants **4**:63–67
  recycling elements **4**:6, 9
  reproduction **1**:8; **4**:18–19; **8**:62–63
bacteriophages **4**:43, 62
balance **7**:57
bats **6**:14, 64; **9**:46
beach zones **5**:67
beer **4**:58
beetles **1**:70; **3**:64; **4**:61; **6**:17, 41, 46, 56
benzene **1**:28–29
bile **7**:14
binary fission **2**:53–54; **4**:18; **8**:9–10
biochemistry **1**:28–37
biodiversity **1**:23; **10**:9
biofeedback **7**:40–41
biological clocks **8**:41
biological control **1**:63; **6**:62
bioluminescence **4**:24
biomes **1**:11; **6**:32; **10**:8–9, 29–36
biosphere **1**:11; **10**:28–29
bird feeders **1**:42
birds **6**:8–9, 11, 12–13, 33, 39; **10**:37
  adaptive radiation **9**:49–50
  care for young **6**:56–57
  defense **6**:47
  eggs **2**:4; **6**:54
  evolution **9**:60; **10**:37
  flight **6**:25–26
  mutualism **6**:58–59
  reproduction **6**:50; **8**:27–28
blood **7**:23, 24–25, 28, 29–31
  cells **2**:10, 15, 59–60; **7**:25, 67, 68–69
  separation **1**:51
bones **2**:16; **7**:34–40
brain **2**:18; **7**:47–54, 57; **8**:58–59
  cancer **2**:67
breathing **7**:26–33
bryophytes **5**:5
budding **1**:8, 9; **8**:8
Burgess Shale **9**:57
butterflies **6**:29, 42; **8**:38, 39–40; **9**:60, 61

C

camouflage **6**:4, 19, 39; **9**:20
cancer **1**:51; **2**:56, 62–70; **3**:19, 58; **8**:67
capillaries **7**:23, 24
captive breeding **10**:68–69
carbohydrates **1**:30–31; **7**:9–10, 13
carbon **1**:29–30; **10**:12–14
carbon dioxide **7**:24, 28, 30; **10**:53
carnivores **6**:10, 12
catabolic reactions **1**:34–35
cats **1**:16, 17, 24–25; **3**:42; **9**:24–25

cells **1**:11; **2**:4–19; **3**:16–17; **8**:67
   communication **2**:44–51
   division **2**:24, 53–61; **3**:6–7, 17, 18–25, 43–44
   internal structure **2**:30–43
   movement **2**:26–29
   support **2**:13, 20–26
cellulose **1**:31; **5**:8–9; **10**:12, 13
centrifuges **1**:51
CFCs **10**:23, 60
Chagas' disease **4**:29, 31
charts **1**:58, 59, 60, 61
cheetahs **6**:17, 24, 69
Chernobyl disaster **10**:57
childbirth **8**:47–50
childhood **8**:58–59
chimpanzees **3**:50; **6**:65
chitin **1**:36
chloroplasts **2**:12, 39–40; **5**:8
cholera **4**:47, 54, 67
chromatin **3**:17–18
chromatography **1**:52, 53, 54
chromosomes **2**:33, 58; **3**:5, 6, 18–25, 39–40, 43–44, 50–53; **8**:9; **9**:28
   abnormalities **3**:57–58
   sex **3**:51–52, 55–56, 57–58
cilates **4**:22, 24, 25, 26
cilia and flagella **2**:27–29
circulatory system **7**:6–7, 18–24
cladistics **1**:18–19
classification **1**:14–20
climate **10**:18–27
clones **1**:64, 65; **3**:66–68; **5**:31, 46, 47
cnidarians **2**:19
coelacanths **6**:8
cold, common **4**:39
color blindness **3**:55
colors **7**:59, 60

commensalisms **6**:60
communication **6**:66–70
communities **1**:11; **10**:7, 8
compost **4**:7
computing **1**:68–70
conifers **5**:21–22
conservation **9**:39, 41; **10**:62–69
continents, moving **9**:12–13
contraception **8**:50
coral reefs **10**:46–47
corals **4**:6, 29; **8**:40, 41
courtship **6**:51; **8**:27
cowbirds **6**:52
cows **10**:12
crabs **6**:39; **8**:35, 37
crayfish **6**:69
creationism **9**:7, 11
crocodiles **6**:8, 23, 54, 58–59
crops **4**:34, 62–63; **5**:44–56, 60
cyanobacteria **4**:12–13, 17; **9**:55
cystic fibrosis **1**:36

D
Darwin, Charles **5**:27–28, 38; **9**:4, 6–7, 16, 17–21, 28, 62; **10**:37, 39
data analysis **1**:58–61
DDT **10**:60
death **2**:29; **7**:50
defense, animal **6**:38–47
deserts **5**:19–21; **6**:31–33; **10**:35–36
detergents, biological **1**:35
detrivores **6**:10, 13
diabetes **1**:31; **2**:44; **3**:65
diapause **6**:29
diaphragm **7**:32–33
diatoms **2**:53; **4**:5, 22, 23, 24, 26, 27
diffusion **7**:27–28

digestive system **7**:7, 11–16
dimorphism, sexual **8**:28; **9**:67
dinoflagellates **4**:22, 23, 24, 27, 28, 29, 30
dinosaurs **2**:16; **6**:9, 24; **9**:8, 58
disease **3**:56–57; **4**:19, 34, 39–40, 44–55, 64; **7**:64, 65–66
dissection **1**:54–55, 56
diversity **6**:4–9; **9**:25
DNA **1**:7; **2**:33; **3**:4, 5, 27–29, 38–39, 46; **9**:15, 28
   bacterial **2**:7; **4**:14–16, 60–61
   comparing **1**:27; **3**:43; **9**:62
   in computing **1**:68–70
   fingerprints **1**:55; **2**:6; **3**:6; **9**:31
   hybridization **1**:26
   junk **3**:39
   mitochondrial **2**:41; **3**:48–49; **9**:68
   protein formation **3**:31–36
   recombinant **3**:63; **4**:60
   replication **3**:18, 29–31, 32
   structure **1**:36, 37; **3**:26, 27, 36; **9**:29, 30
dodos **9**:53
dogs **1**:26; **3**:46; **6**:70
dolphins **6**:14, 70; **9**:59
domestication **3**:61
dominance **6**:67
drugs **4**:51, 54; **5**:49
   designer **1**:66–67
   recreational **5**:49–50

E
ears and hearing **6**:13; **7**:60–62
Earth **10**:29
echolocation **6**:14, 42–43
ecology **10**:4–9
ecosystems **1**:10–12; **10**:7, 28–39, 30, 40–49

ecotourism **10**:61
eggs **2**:4; **6**:52–54; **8**:19, 24, 32–33, 34, 43; **9**:50
electric fields **6**:15, 67
electrophoresis **1**:53–54, 55
elements **1**:28, 29
elephants **1**:27; **6**:68
embryos **1**:24; **8**:54, 55
endocrine system **2**:48; **7**:54–55; **8**:59–60
endoplasmic reticulum **2**:33–35, 46
energy **2**:42; **10**:10–11, 61
enzymes **1**:33, 34–35; **3**:29; **4**:58–59
  digestive **7**:11, 13–14
  restriction **4**:60–61
epithelium **2**:14–15
ergonomics **1**:70
esophagus **7**:13
estivation **6**:31
estrus cycle **8**:23–24
euglenoids **4**:22, 25
eukaryotes **1**:14, 15–16; **2**:7, 8–9, 30–31, 53; **4**:9, 21–23; **9**:55–56
evolution **9**:4–15, 35–40, 44–53, 54–61
  convergent **1**:20, 21; **9**:11–12, 14, 51–53, 59
  eukaryote **2**:7
  genetics and **9**:26–31
  human **3**:59; **9**:62–70
  on islands **10**:37
  iterative **9**:52
  rates **9**:10, 42
excretion **1**:7; **7**:8, 17
experiments **1**:39, 41, 56, 59–60
extinctions **9**:53, 57, 58; **10**:54, 69–70
eyes **7**:57–60; **9**:27

F
falcons, peregrine **10**:68–69
farming **1**:62–63; **3**:60, 61, 64; **5**:18, 45; **10**:50–51, 60
fats **1**:32; **7**:10, 14
feeding **1**:7; **6**:10–19
fermentation **4**:10, 57–58
fertilization **8**:19, 25–27
  in vitro **2**:54
  plant **5**:37–39, 40
  self **8**:15
fertilizers **10**:15, 16, 48
fetuses **2**:18; **8**:55, 59
fiber **5**:54–55
field studies **1**:38–47, 58
finches, Galápagos **9**:17, 49–50; **10**:37
fires **5**:22
fish **6**:8, 15, 19, 36, 37, 59
  deep-sea **10**:44–45
  defense **6**:46–47
  evolution **9**:57–58
  flying **6**:38–39
  fossil **9**:7
  reproduction **6**:53; **8**:4, 16, 26
  swimming **6**:22–23
fishing **10**:42
flagellates **4**:22, 29
Fleming, Alexander **4**:19
flies **1**:5, 70; **8**:37; **9**:28
flight **6**:25–27
flowers **1**:56; **5**:34, 37, 38, 43, 56, 57
food **2**:42; **5**:69; **7**:8–11, 24, 65
  from microorganisms **4**:10, 56–59
  genetically modified **3**:62, 66; **4**:60; **6**:22
food chains and webs **4**:6; **5**:6; **10**:4–5, 6, 41

foraminiferans **4**:22, 23, 25
forests **6**:33–35; **10**:8, 34–35
  see also rainforests
fossils **1**:22; **4**:25; **9**:7, 8, 9–11, 42, 57
  imprints **9**:56
  looking for **9**:61
  tracks **9**:66
founder effect **9**:38–39
foxes, fennec **6**:31
freshwater habitats **6**:37; **10**:48–49
frogs **6**:23–24; **8**:25
fruit, ripening **5**:29–30
fuels **4**:69–70; **10**:14
fungi **1**:21; **2**:9; **4**:44–45; **5**:5, 13

G
Gaia hypothesis **10**:65
Galen, Claudius **7**:5, 6–7
galls **6**:46
gas exchange **7**:24, 28–29
gender **3**:51; **8**:20–21, 29
gene flow **9**:37, 39–40
gene pools **1**:23; **9**:29, 36, 37
gene probes **3**:46
genera **1**:16, 17
genes **2**:33; **3**:4–5, 6, 7, 11, 27–29, 34, 38–39; **8**:16–18; **9**:20, 26, 28, 29, 32–33
  compared **1**:26, 27
  control of **2**:12, 66–67; **3**:36–37, 47; **8**:56–57
  interaction **3**:40–41
  linked **3**:14, 40, 55–56
  mapping **3**:58–59
  testing **3**:55
gene therapy **2**:68; **3**:68–70
genetic disorders **9**:31
genetic drift **9**:26, 36–37, 39

genetic engineering **3**:63–66; **4**:59–63, 68; **5**:30–31
genetic modification (GM) **1**:64; **3**:7; **4**:60, 62–63, 66–67; **5**:34
genetics **3**:4–7
 applied **3**:60–70
 human **3**:50–59; **9**:40
 population **9**:32–43
genomes **3**:5, 38–49, 50–52
genotypes **3**:11, 42–43, 54–55
gestation **6**:55
gliding **6**:25, 26
global warming **10**:24, 25, 53, 58–59
glucose **1**:30, 31, 34, 35
glue, casein **1**:32
glycerol **1**:32
glycogen **1**:31; **7**:16
Golgi apparatus **2**:35
gorillas **6**:64, 65
grafting **5**:47
Gram stain **2**:23; **4**:15
graphs **1**:60–61
grasses **5**:18
grasslands **6**:35; **10**:33
greenhouse gases **10**:23–24, 58, 59
Green Revolution **1**:62
group living **6**:47, 62–65
growth **1**:9; **8**:57–61
guano **10**:16–17

H
habitats **1**:11; **6**:28–29, 32; **10**:5–6, 8
 loss **10**:51–53, 66
Haeckel, Ernst **1**:24
handedness **7**:52
healing **3**:18
heart **7**:18, 19–23
heart attacks **2**:46

heart disease **7**:24
height **9**:27
hemoglobin **1**:25, 33; **7**:24, 30, 31
hemophilia **3**:56
hepatitis **4**:42–43, 50
herbivores **6**:10–12, 13
herds **6**:47, 62–63; **9**:52
hermaphrodites **6**:49; **8**:20–21
hibernation **6**:28–29; **9**:24
HIV/AIDS **4**:33, 37–38, 40, 41, 46–47, 50, 55; **7**:70; **8**:53
homeostasis **7**:7
honeybees **6**:70
hoof-and-mouth disease **4**:46
Hooke, Robert **2**:5
hormones **1**:33; **2**:48–49; **7**:10, 54–55; **8**:22–23, 47, 59–60, 69
 plant **5**:24–31
horses, evolution **9**:10, 11
HRT **8**:69
human development **8**:54–61
Human Genome Project **3**:7, 15, 45, 58–59
humors **1**:4
hunting **6**:17–19
Huxley, Thomas **9**:7
hybrids **1**:17; **3**:62–63; **9**:45
hydras **8**:8
hydrothermal vents **10**:45
hypothalamus **7**:50, 55; **8**:60
hypotheses **1**:39, 59, 61

I
immune system **4**:49; **7**:25, 64, 66–70
immunization and vaccines **1**:66; **4**:40, 42, 49–51, 67; **7**:64, 65, 67, 68
imprinting **6**:57

inbreeding **9**:40–42
infertility **8**:50–51, 52
inflammatory response **7**:66, 67, 68
inheritance **3**:8–15
insects **1**:70; **6**:6, 14, 37
 eggs **6**:52–53
 exoskeleton **1**:36; **7**:36
 flight **6**:25, 26
 growth **8**:38–39
 mimicry by **6**:40
 nighttime **1**:44
 social **6**:63
insulin **1**:31, 33; **2**:48; **3**:40, 65–66; **4**:68; **8**:65
intestines **7**:14–15
introns and exons **3**:34
invertebrates **6**:6–7; **8**:12–13, 23
islands **9**:38; **10**:37–38

J
jellyfish **6**:6, 16, 22; **8**:36
Jenner, Edward **1**:66; **4**:50
joints **7**:34–35, 39–40

K
kangaroos **6**:24, 55
karyotypes **3**:22, 39–40
Kekulé, Friedrich A. **1**:28–29
kidneys **7**:17
Koch, Robert **1**:54; **4**:5, 47, 55

L
laboratory methods **1**:48–57
Lamarckism **9**:5–6, 16
language, human **6**:70
larvae **8**:36, 37, 38
learning **7**:53
leaves **2**:12–13; **5**:10, 11–12, 26, 29
Leeuwenhoek, Anton van **4**:5, 50

lichens **8**:11
life **1**:4–13, 10, 30; **9**:54–61
life cycles **8**:10, 30–41
life expectancy **7**:64–65; **8**:63–67
ligaments **7**:40
Linnaeus, Carolus **1**:14, 16
lipids **1**:32, 36
Lister, Joseph **4**:52
liver **7**:16
lizards **6**:20, 22, 33, 44; **8**:14
Lorenzo's oil **2**:43
"Lucy" skeleton **9**:65
lungs **2**:62; **7**:28–29, 31–32, 33, 65; **8**:68
lymphatic system **7**:68, 69–70
lymphocytes **7**:69, 70
lysosomes **2**:37–38

M
malaria **4**:30, 31, 45, 52, 53, 54
mammals **1**:24; **6**:9, 55–56; **9**:60–61
  forelimbs **1**:25, 26
  reproduction **1**:8; **6**:55; **8**:28–29
mantises **6**:51, 52
Mars **1**:13; **4**:70
marsupials **9**:12–13, 51, 52
mating **6**:51–52; **8**:27–29
measles **4**:40, 41
medicine **1**:65–67
meiosis **2**:60–61; **3**:7, 21–25, 43–44, 52–53; **9**:28, 34
memory **7**:53–54
Mendel, Gregor **3**:8–15, 26; **9**:20–21, 28
menopause **8**:69–70
menstrual cycle **8**:23–24, 45
metabolism **1**:35
metamorphosis **8**:38–39
metazoans **9**:56–57

meteorites, from Mars **1**:13
mice **9**:23
microorganisms **1**:9; **4**:4–7, 44–55, 56–70
  in the gut **4**:6; **6**:12, 59
microscopes **1**:6, 49–51; **2**:5
migrations **6**:29
milk **6**:55–56
mimicry **6**:39–40, 41–42, 43, 46
mind, theory of **6**:65
minerals **7**:10–11; **10**:17
miscarriage **8**:50–51
mites **6**:25, 60
mitochondria **2**:7, 41–42
mitosis **2**:56–58; **3**:7, 18–20
moas **9**:25
molecules **1**:10, 11, 28
monkeys **6**:68, 69; **9**:23
monosaccharides **1**:30, 31; **7**:9
mosquitoes **4**:30, 45, 52, 53; **6**:61–62
mosses **8**:10, 12
moths **6**:39, 42–43, 68
mountains **6**:30; **10**:20–21, 32–33
movement **1**:7–8; **4**:17–18; **6**:20–27
multiple fission **8**:10
multiple sclerosis **2**:51
muscles **2**:16–17, 20, 29; **6**:20; **7**:40–43
  cardiac **7**:18–19, 42
mushrooms **3**:48; **8**:10
mutations **2**:63–67; **4**:55; **9**:21–22, 29–31, 35, 43
mutualism **4**:6; **6**:58, 70

N
nails **2**:52
names, scientific **1**:16; **9**:44
neo-Darwinism **9**:22

nerves **7**:45, 48
nervous system **7**:27, 44–54, 55
neurons (nerve cells) **2**:17–18, 51, 61; **7**:44, 45, 46, 48
newts **6**:41
niches **10**:6–7
nitrogen **4**:6, 9; **5**:17; **10**:14–16, 22
nocturnal animals **6**:15
nose **7**:63, 67
nucleic acids **1**:35–37
  see also DNA; RNA
nucleotides **1**:27, 36; **3**:27
nucleus **2**:32–33

O
oceans **6**:35–37, 49; **10**:41–48, 58
oil spills **4**:64; **10**:59
omnivores **6**:10, 11
organelles **1**:16; **2**:8–9, 30, 33–43; **3**:17
organization, biological **1**:10–13
organs **1**:10, 11; **2**:6; **7**:5
osmosis **4**:28
osteoporosis **7**:38; **8**:68, 69
oxygen **5**:10; **7**:23–24, 27–28, 30–31; **10**:22
ozone layer **9**:55; **10**:23

P
pacemakers, heart **1**:65–66
pain **7**:46
painkillers **2**:48
pancreas **2**:48
pandas **6**:11; **10**:70
pandemics **4**:46
parasites **4**:29; **5**:19; **6**:12, 60–62; **8**:33; **9**:61
parental care **8**:33–36
Parkinson's disease **2**:50
parthenogenesis **8**:13–14, 15, 18

Pasteur, Louis **4**:5, 47, 50, 67
peacocks **8**:28; **9**:18
pedomorphosis **8**:38
penicillin **4**:19
peristalsis **7**:13
peroxisomes **2**:38–39
pest control **1**:63; **3**:64; **4**:38, 61, 63; **6**:62
pesticides **10**:60, 68
phagocytes **4**:48; **7**:66, 68–69, 70
phenotype **3**:11
pheromones **6**:68, 69
phloem **2**:14; **5**:10–11
phosphorus **10**:16–17
photosynthesis **4**:13, 24; **5**:4, 7, 10; **10**:10
Piltdown Man **9**:64
pituitary gland **7**:49, 54, 55; **8**:60
plankton **4**:27, 28; **6**:30; **8**:36–37; **10**:41, 42
plants **1**:6, 22; **5**:1–23
   cells **2**:8, 9, 11–14, 22–23, 38, 46, 59; **3**:20; **5**:4–5, 6–9
   cloned **3**:66–67; **5**:31
   counting **1**:46
   hormones **5**:24–31
   parasites **5**:19
   and people **5**:44–57
   reproduction and propagation **5**:32–43; **8**:10–12, 22
   sensitivity **1**:9
   viruses **4**:38–39
   water plants **10**:12
plasmids **3**:63–64; **4**:16, 55, 60–61
plastics, biodegradable **1**:37; **4**:65
plovers **6**:54, 58–59
pneumonia **4**:37
polar regions **6**:28, 29–31, 36; **10**:30–31, 58–59
polio **4**:34, 37, 39–40, 50

pollen and pollination **5**:34, 35–37, 40; **8**:10, 18
pollution **4**:63–67; **5**:12; **6**:36; **7**:30; **10**:36, 56–61
polymerase chain reaction **3**:37
polypeptides **1**:33
polyploids **3**:25, 38, 44, 61; **9**:47–48
ponds **6**:37; **10**:49
populations **1**:11; **10**:7, 38–39
   genetics **9**:32–43
Portuguese man-o'-war **6**:63
predators **6**:12–13, 14–16, 17; **10**:38–39
pregnancy **8**:45–48
primates **6**:64–65; **9**:62
prions **4**:42
prokaryotes **1**:14, 16; **2**:7, 30, 52, 53–54; **4**:9; **9**:55
prostheses **7**:41
proteins **1**:10, 32–34, 36; **3**:5, 29, 31–36; **7**:9
protists **2**:9; **4**:4–6, 20–31; **8**:9, 17
protozoa **4**:21
puberty **8**:61
punctuated equilibria **9**:42–43
Punnett squares **3**:10

Q
quadrats **1**:40

R
rabies **4**:50
radiolarians **4**:22, 23, 25, 28–29
rain, acid **10**:58
rainforests **1**:46; **6**:34–35; **10**:34–35, 53
recombination **9**:33–34
red tides **4**:30
reflexes **7**:47

remora fish **6**:60
reproduction **1**:9; **6**:48–57; **8**:4–7, 42–53
   asexual **1**:8; **4**:18, 27; **5**:32–33, 35; **6**:48; **8**:5, 8–15
   sexual **1**:8; **4**:26; **5**:33–35; **6**:48, 49–50; **8**:4–5, 16–29; **9**:51
reptiles **6**:8, 23; **9**:50, 58–60
reserves, ecological **10**:66–67
respiration **1**:7, 34–35; **7**:31; **10**:14
respiratory system **7**:28–29
ribosomes **2**:34
RNA **1**:7, 36, 37; **2**:33; **3**:31, 32–36, 58
robots **7**:55
root nodules **10**:16
roots **5**:13, 20, 24, 29
roundworms **8**:65
rubber **5**:55
ruminants **9**:50–51

S
saliva **7**:12, 13
sampling **1**:42–45
sandgrouse **6**:33
sargassum **5**:63
scavengers **6**:12
SCID **3**:69–70
scorpions **6**:15, 51; **8**:23
scrublands **10**:35–36
sea cucumbers **6**:45
sea hares **6**:45
seahorses **6**:53; **8**:26
sea levels **10**:24
seals **1**:12, 13, 26
sea mice **1**:68
seashores **10**:46, 47–48
seasons **10**:20–21
sea urchins **8**:65
seawater **10**:40

seaweeds **5**:5, 58–70
seeds **1**:8, 9; **5**:39–40, 41, 46; **8**:5
selection
  artificial **9**:6, 21
  natural **9**:4–5, 6, 16–25, 35, 36
  sexual **9**:18
selective breeding **1**:63–64;
  3:60–63; **8**:6, 7
senses **1**:9; **6**:13–15; **7**:56–63
sensitivity **1**:9
sewage treatment **4**:13, 66, 67
sharks **6**:19, 35
sheep **3**:67–68; **9**:6, 52
shells **6**:44–45
silicon, life based on **1**:30
skeletons **1**:36; **7**:34–35, 36, 38–39
  hydrostatic **6**:20–22
skin **2**:31, 65; **7**:67
sleeping sickness **4**:29, 30–31
slugs **6**:23, 49
smallpox **1**:66; **4**:40, 41, 45–46, 50, 51, 67
smell, sense of **6**:14; **7**:62–63
smoking **5**:51; **7**:32, 65
snails **1**:44; **6**:16–17, 21, 23, 44–45
snakes **6**:8, 14–15, 16, 43, 54
  hind limbs **1**:26, 27; **9**:15
social groups **8**:28–29
soil **10**:27
sound **6**:43, 68
species **1**:14–15, 17, 20–25, 45; **9**:45–46
  cryptic **9**:46
  genetic markers **1**:27
  indicator **10**:10
  introduced **5**:56; **10**:55
  new **9**:38, 39, 42–43, 45, 46–48
  plant **5**:33
  rainforest **1**:46
sperm **2**:11; **8**:19, 24–25, 27, 42, 44

spiders **6**:16, 19, 21, 47, 68
  reproduction **6**:51–52, 53; **8**:27
spinal cord **7**:45, 46
sponges **2**:18–19; **8**:13
spontaneous generation **1**:5; **4**:47; **9**:5
spores **5**:32–33; **8**:10, 11–12
sporozoans **4**:22
squid **6**:22, 45, 59
starch **1**:31
STDs **8**:51–53
stem cells **2**:18, 60; **8**:56
stems **2**:13; **5**:12–13, 16
steroids **1**:32; **7**:43
stomach **7**:7, 13–14
stromatolites **1**:22
sugar **2**:48; **5**:48
surveys **1**:43
symbiosis **4**:6, 28–29; **6**:58–62
symmetry **6**:4–5
systems, body **1**:10, 11; **7**:4–7

T
tails **9**:12
tapeworms **6**:5, 12, 60, 61
Tasmanian wolves **10**:54
taste **7**:13, 62, 63
teeth **7**:12
tendons **7**:42
thalamus **7**:49
tigers **6**:66–67
time, geological **9**:55
tissues **1**:10, 11; **7**:4–5
toads **6**:18, 46–47, 53; **10**:55
tongue **7**:13, 63
tortoises, giant **3**:49; **9**:17–18
touch **7**:56–57
tracking **1**:45–47
transpiration **5**:8, 9

transplants **7**:18, 23, 49
traps **1**:40, 41, 44
tree rings **10**:25
trees **5**:12–13, 15, 27, 52–53; **8**:30
trophic levels **10**:11
tropisms **5**:28–29
trypanosomes **4**:29, 30–31
tuberculosis **4**:52–53
tundras **6**:30; **10**:31–32
turtles **8**:21; **10**:52, 69
twins **3**:53–54; **8**:46–47; **9**:34

V
vacuoles **2**:35–37, 38
variation **3**:22, 41; **9**:21–22, 27
veins **7**:23, 24
ventilators **7**:32
vertebrates **6**:7–9; **9**:57–58
vestigial features **1**:26–27; **9**:12, 15
viroids **4**:34
viruses **1**:7; **3**:35, 64; **4**:6–7, 32–43, 34, 44, 55
  and cancer **2**:64
  computer **4**:43
vitamins **7**:10

W
wasps, parasitic **1**:63; **6**:47, 62
water **10**:26–27
weeds **8**:12, 31–32; **9**:25
wetlands **10**:49, 52
whales **6**:17, 23, 56; **9**:15, 42; **10**:43
whaling **10**:54, 65, 67
wood **5**:52–53
worms **6**:5, 12, 21, 49

X, Y
xylem **2**:13–14; **5**:9–10
yeast **1**:10; **4**:56–57, 58